THE Secret OF THE Swan

Seeing Yourself through God's Eyes

GLORIA CHISHOLM

Augsburg

MINNEAPOLIS

To the swans who glided,
causing me to look down and see my reflection;
you know who you are.

THE SECRET OF THE SWAN
Seeing Yourself through God's Eyes

Cover design: Peggy Lauritsen Design Group
Interior design: Virginia Aretz, Northwestern Printcrafters

Library of Congress Cataloging-in-Publication Data

Chisholm, Gloria
    The secret of the swan : seeing yourself through God's eyes /
Gloria Chisholm.
        p.   cm.
    Includes bibliographical references.
    ISBN 0-8066-2671-2 :
    1. God—Love.   2. Love—Religious aspects—Christianity.   3. Self-
acceptance—Religious aspects—Christianity.   4. Forgiveness—
Religious aspects—Christianity.   I. Title.
    BT140.C48   1993
    248.4—dc20   93-22406
                                                                            CIP

Manufactured in the U.S.A.   AF 9–2671

97   96   95   94   93   1   2   3   4   5   6   7   8   9   10

Contents

Preface

"What do you want to be when you grow up?" is a question that many grown-ups (whose dreams may have died long ago) like to ask little kids. Children enthusiastically reply: "An astronaut." "A rock star." "The president of the United States."

I wanted to be a nun. A flight attendant. A psychologist. An actress. A writer.

When I made some poor choices along the way and realized that I might not amount to anything at all, I was crushed. My hopes and dreams were dying faster than I could bury them.

As I watched my dreams slip away one by one, I began to identify more and more with one of my favorite fairy-tale characters—the ugly duckling. This little guy experienced a number of life-threatening mishaps because no one valued him, understood him, or even liked him. They didn't know what he really was or what he was about to become. Even *he* didn't know the truth about himself—until the lovely birds recognized him as one of their own.

Like the ugly duckling, I have often felt devalued, misunderstood, or not liked. Sometimes the more I have let others see and experience the "real" me, the more they have turned up their noses, judged me, hurt me, or tried to get me to change.

Have you ever felt that way? Have you had trouble finding genuine love and acceptance? Why is it that so many of us feel like such ugly ducklings so much of the time?

It's nothing short of a miracle when we see our true reflections in the pond's still waters. This is the moment when we realize we were created in God's own image. We may feel like ugly ducklings, but the swan we see reflected in the water is the resurrected Christ who dwells in us. The challenge is being able to accept the truth about who we are.

The journey taken by the ugly duckling is available to each of us. But how can we unravel the secret of our true identity? How do we come to see ourselves the way God sees us? And how can we learn to act like the swans God created us to be? These are the questions that led me to write this book.

What do you want to be when you grow up? Have you ever, in your wildest dreams, imagined that God created you to be a swan?

The Ugly Duckling

by Hans Christian Andersen

It was so beautiful out in the country. It was summer. The oats were still green, but the wheat was turning yellow. Down in the meadow the grass had been cut and made into haystacks; and there the storks walked on their long red legs talking Egyptian, because that was the language they had been taught by their mothers. The fields were enclosed by woods, and hidden among them were little lakes and pools. Yes, it certainly was lovely out there in the country!

The old castle, with its deep moat surrounding it, lay bathed in sunshine. Between the heavy walls and the edge of the moat there was a narrow strip of land covered by a whole forest of burdock plants. Their leaves were large and some of the stalks were so tall that a child could stand upright under them and imagine that he was in the middle of the wild and lonesome woods. Here a duck had built her nest. While she sat waiting for the eggs to hatch, she felt a little sorry for herself because it was taking so long and hardly anybody came to visit her. The other ducks preferred swimming in the moat to sitting under a dock leaf and gossiping.

Finally the eggs began to crack. "Peep . . . Peep," they said one after another. The egg yolks had become alive and were sticking out their heads.

"Quack . . . Quack . . . " said their mother. "Look around you." And the ducklings did; they glanced at the green world about them, and that was what their mother wanted them to do, for green was good for their eyes.

"How big the world is!" piped the little ones, for they had much more space to move around in now than they had had inside the egg.

"Do you think that this is the whole world?" quacked their mother. "The world is much larger than this. It stretches as far as the minister's wheat fields, though I have not been there. . . . Are you all here?" The duck got up and turned around to look at her nest. "Oh no, the biggest egg hasn't hatched yet; and I'm so tired of sitting here! I wonder how long it will take?" she wailed, and sat down again.

"What's new?" asked an old duck who had come visiting.

"One of the eggs is taking so long," complained the mother duck. "It won't crack. But take a look at the others. They are the sweetest little ducklings you have ever seen; and every one of them looks exactly like their father. That scoundrel hasn't come to visit me once."

"Let me look at the egg that won't hatch," demanded the old duck. "I am sure that it's a turkey egg! I was fooled that way once. You can't imagine what it's like. Turkeys are afraid of the water. I couldn't get them to go into it. I quacked and I nipped them, but nothing helped. Let me see that egg! . . . Yes, it's a turkey egg. Just let it lie there. You go and teach your young ones how to swim, that's my advice."

"I have sat on it so long that I guess I can sit a little longer, at least until they get the hay in," replied the mother duck.

"Suit yourself," said the older duck, and went on.

At last the big egg cracked too. "Peep . . . Peep," said the young one, and tumbled out. He was big and very ugly.

The mother duck looked at him. "He's awfully big for his age," she said. "He doesn't look like any of the others. I wonder if he could be a turkey? Well, we shall soon see. Into the water he will go, even if I have to kick him to make him do it."

The next day the weather was gloriously beautiful. The sun shone on the forest of burdock plants. The mother duck took her whole brood to the moat. "Quack . . . Quack . . . " she ordered.

One after another, the little ducklings plunged into the water. For a moment their heads disappeared, but then they popped up again and the little ones floated like so many corks. Their legs knew what to do without being told. All of the new brood swam very nicely, even the ugly one.

"He is no turkey," mumbled the mother. "See how beautifully he uses his legs and how straight he holds his neck. He is my own child and, when you look closely at him, he's quite handsome . . . .Quack! Quack! Follow me and I'll take you to the henyard and introduce you to everyone. But stay close to me, so that no one steps on you, and look out for the cat."

They heard an awful noise when they arrived at the henyard. Two families of ducks had got into a fight over the head of an eel. Neither of them got it, for it was swiped by the cat.

"That is the way of the world," said the mother duck, and licked her bill. She would have liked to have the eel's head herself. "Walk nicely," she admonished them. "And remember to bow to the old duck over there. She has Spanish blood in her veins and is the most aristocratic fowl here. That is why she is so fat and has a red rag tied around one of her legs. That is the highest mark of distinction a duck can be given. It means so much that she will never be done away with; and all the other fowl and the human beings know who she is. Quack! Quack! . . . Don't walk, waddle like well-brought-up ducklings. Keep your legs far apart, just as your mother and father have always done. Bow your heads and say, 'Quack!' " And that was what the little ducklings did.

Other ducks gathered about them and said loudly, "What do we want that gang here for? Aren't there enough of us already? Pooh! Look how ugly one of them is! He's the last straw!" And one of the ducks flew over and bit the ugly duckling on the neck.

"Leave him alone!" shouted the mother. "He hasn't done anyone any harm."

"He's big and he doesn't look like everybody else!" replied the duck who had bitten him. "And that's reason enough to beat him."

"Very good-looking children you have," remarked the duck with the red rag around one of her legs. "All of them are beautiful except one. He didn't turn out very well. I wish you could make him over again."

"That's not possible, Your Grace," answered the mother duck. "He may not be handsome, but he has a good character and swims as well as the others, if not a little better. Perhaps he will grow handsomer as he grows older and becomes a bit smaller. He was in the egg too long, and that is why he doesn't have the right shape." She smoothed his neck for a moment and then added, "Besides, he's a drake; and it doesn't matter so much what he looks like. He is strong and I am sure he will be able to take care of himself."

"Well, the others are nice," said the old duck. "Make yourself at home, and if you should find an eel's head, you may bring it to me."

And they were "at home."

The poor little duckling, who had been the last to hatch and was so ugly, was bitten and pushed and made fun of both by the hens and by the other ducks. The turkey cock (who had been born with spurs on, and therefore thought he was an emperor) rustled his feathers as if he were a full-rigged ship under sail, and strutted up to the duckling. He gobbled so loudly at him that his own face got all red.

The poor little duckling did not know where to turn. How he grieved over his own ugliness, and how sad he was! The poor creature was mocked and laughed at by the whole hen-yard.

That was the first day; and each day that followed was worse than the one before. The poor duckling was chased and mistreated by everyone, even his own sisters and brothers, who quacked again and again, "If only the cat would get you, you ugly thing!"

Even his mother said, "I wish you were far away." The other ducks bit him and the hens pecked at him. The little girl who came to feed the fowls kicked him.

At last the duckling ran away. It flew over the tops of the bushes, frightening all the little birds so that they flew up into the air. "They, too, think I am ugly," thought the duckling, and closed his eyes — but he kept on running.

Finally he came to a great swamp where wild ducks lived; and here he stayed for the night, for he was too tired to go any farther.

In the morning he was discovered by the wild ducks. They looked at him and one of them asked, "What kind of bird are you?"

The ugly duckling bowed in all directions, for he was trying to be as polite as he knew how.

"You are ugly," said the wild ducks, "but that is no concern of ours, as long as you don't try to marry into our family."

The poor duckling wasn't thinking of marriage. All he wanted was to be allowed to swim among the reeds and drink a little water when he was thirsty.

He spent two days in the swamp; then two wild geese came —or rather, two wild ganders, for they were males. They had been hatched not long ago; therefore they were both frank and bold.

"Listen, comrade," they said. "You are so ugly that we like you. Do you want to migrate with us? Not far from here there is a marsh where some beautiful wild geese live. They are all lovely maidens, and you are so ugly that you may seek your fortune among them. Come along."

"Bang! Bang!" Two shots were heard and both the ganders fell down dead among the reeds, and the water turned red from their blood.

"Bang! Bang!" Again came the sound of shots, and a flock of wild geese flew up.

The whole swamp was surrounded by hunters; from every direction came the awful noise. Some of the hunters had hidden behind bushes or among the reeds but others, screened from sight by the leaves, sat on the long, low branches of the trees that stretched out over the swamp. The blue smoke from the guns lay like a fog over the water and among the trees. Dogs came splashing through the marsh, and they bent and broke the reeds.

The poor little duckling was terrified. He was about to tuck his head under his wing, in order to hide, when he saw a big dog peering at him through the reeds. The dog's tongue hung out of its mouth and its eyes glistened evilly. It bared its teeth. Splash! It turned away without touching the duckling.

"Oh, thank God!" he sighed. "I am so ugly that even the dog doesn't want to bite me."

The little duckling lay as still as he could while the shots whistled through the reeds. Not until the middle of the afternoon did the shooting stop; but the poor little duckling was still so frightened that he waited several hours longer before taking his head out from under his wing. Then he ran as quickly as he could out of the swamp. Across the fields and the meadows he went, but a wind had come up and he found it hard to make his way against it.

Toward evening he came upon a poor little hut. It was so wretchedly crooked that it looked as if it couldn't make up its mind which way to fall and that was why it was still standing. The wind was blowing so hard that the poor little duckling had to sit down in order not to be blown away. Suddenly he noticed that the door was off its hinges, making a crack; and he squeezed himself through it and was inside.

An old woman lived in the hut with her cat and her hen. The cat was called Sonny and could both arch his back and purr. Oh yes, it could also make sparks if you rubbed its fur the wrong way. The hen had very short legs and that was why she was called Cluck Lowlegs. But she was good at laying eggs, and the old woman loved her as if she were her own child.

In the morning the hen and the cat discovered the duckling. The cat meowed and the hen clucked.

"What is going on?" asked the old woman, and looked around. She couldn't see very well, and when she found the duckling she thought it was a fat, full-grown duck. "What a fine catch!" she exclaimed. "Now we shall have duck eggs, unless it's a drake. We'll give it a try."

So the duckling was allowed to stay for three weeks on probation, but he laid no eggs. The cat was the master of the house and the hen the mistress. They always referred to themselves as "we and the world," for they thought that they were half the world—and the better half at that. The duckling thought that he should be allowed to have a different opinion, but the hen did not agree.

"Can you lay eggs?" she demanded.

"No," answered the duckling.

"Then keep your mouth shut."

And the cat asked, "Can you arch your back? Can you purr? Can you make sparks?"

"No."

"Well, in that case, you have no right to have an opinion when sensible people are talking."

The duckling was sitting in a corner and was in a bad mood. Suddenly he recalled how lovely it could be outside in the fresh air when the sun shone: a great longing to be floating in the water came over the duckling, and he could not help talking about it.

"What is the matter with you?" asked the hen as soon as she had heard what he had to say. "You have nothing to do, that's why you get ideas like that. Lay eggs or purr, and such notions will disappear."

"You have no idea how delightful it is to float in the water, and to dive down to the bottom of a lake and get your head wet," said the duckling.

"Yes, that certainly does sound amusing," said the hen. "You must have gone mad. Ask the cat—he is the most intelligent being I know—ask him whether he likes to swim or dive down to the bottom of a lake. Don't take my word for anything. . . .Ask the old woman, who is the cleverest person in the world; ask her whether she likes to float and to get her head all wet."

"You don't understand me!" wailed the duckling.

"And if I don't understand you, who will? I hope you don't think that you are wiser than the cat or the old woman—not to mention myself. Don't give yourself airs! Thank your Creator for all He has done for you. Aren't you sitting in a warm room among intelligent people whom you could learn something from? While you, yourself, do nothing but say a lot of nonsense and aren't the least bit amusing! Believe me, that's the truth, and I am only telling it to you for your own good. That's how you recognize a true friend; it's someone who is willing to tell you the truth, no matter how unpleasant it is. Now get to work: lay some eggs, or learn to purr and arch your back."

"I think I'll go out into the wide world," replied the duckling.

"Go right ahead!" said the hen.

And the duckling left. He found a lake where he could float in the water and dive to the bottom. There were other ducks, but they ignored him because he was so ugly.

Autumn came and the leaves turned yellow and brown, then they fell from the trees. The wind caught them and made them dance. The clouds were heavy with hail and snow. A raven sat on a fence and screeched, "Ach! Ach!" because it was so cold. When just thinking of how cold it was is enough to make one shiver, what a terrible time the duckling must have had.

One evening just as the sun was setting gloriously, a flock of beautiful birds came out from among the rushes. Their feathers were so white that they glistened; and they had long, graceful necks. They were swans. They made a very loud cry, then they spread their powerful wings. They were flying south to a warmer climate, where the lakes were not frozen in the winter. Higher and higher they circled. The ugly duckling turned round and round in the water like a wheel and stretched his neck up toward the sky; he felt a strange longing. He screeched so piercingly that he frightened himself.

Oh, he would never forget those beautiful birds, those happy birds. When they were out of sight the duckling dove down under the water to the bottom of the lake; and when he came up again he was beside himself. He did not know the name of those birds or where they were going, and yet he felt that he loved them as he had never loved any other creatures. He did not envy them. It did not even occur to him to wish that he were so handsome himself. He would have been happy if the other ducks had let him stay in the henyard: that poor, ugly bird!

The weather grew colder and colder. The duckling had to swim round and round in the water, to keep just a little space for himself that wasn't frozen. Each night his hole became smaller and smaller. On all sides of him the ice creaked and groaned. The little duckling had to keep his feet constantly in motion so that the last bit of open water wouldn't become ice. At last he was too tired to swim any more. He sat still. The ice closed in around him and he was frozen fast.

Early the next morning a farmer saw him and with his clogs broke the ice to free the duckling. The man put the bird under his arm and took it home to his wife, who brought the duckling back to life.

The children wanted to play with him. But the duckling was afraid that they were going to hurt him, so he flapped his wings and flew right into the milk pail. From there he flew into a big bowl of butter and then into a barrel of flour. What a sight he was!

The farmer's wife yelled and chased him with a poker. The children laughed and almost fell on top of each other, trying to catch him; and how they screamed! Luckily for the duckling, the door was open. He got out of the house and found a hiding place beneath some bushes, in the newly fallen snow; and there he lay so still, as though there were hardly any life left in him.

It would be too horrible to tell of all the hardship and suffering the duckling experienced that long winter. It is enough to know that he did survive. When again the sun shone warmly and the larks began to sing, the duckling was lying among the reeds in the swamp. Spring had come!

He spread out his wings to fly. How strong and powerful they were! Before he knew it, he was far from the swamp and flying above a beautiful garden. The apple trees were blooming and the lilac bushes stretched their flower-covered branches over the water of a winding canal. Everything was so beautiful: so fresh and green. Out of a forest of rushes came three swans. They ruffled their feathers and floated so lightly on the water. The ugly duckling recognized the birds and felt again that strange sadness come over him.

"I shall fly over to them, those royal birds! And they can hack me to death because I, who am so ugly, dare to approach them! What difference does it make? It is better to be killed by them than to be bitten by the other ducks, and pecked by the hens, and kicked by the girl who tends the henyard; or to suffer through the winter."

And he lighted on the water and swam toward the magnificent swans. When they saw him they ruffled their feathers and started to swim in his direction. They were coming to meet him.

"Kill me," whispered the poor creature, and bent his head humbly while he waited for death. But what was that he saw in the water? It was his own reflection; and he was no longer an awkward, clumsy, gray bird, so ungainly and so ugly. He was a swan!

It does not matter that one has been born in the henyard as long as one has lain in a swan's egg.

He was thankful that he had known so much want, and gone through so much suffering, for it made him appreciate his present happiness and the loveliness of everything about him all the more. The swans made a circle around him and caressed him with their beaks.

Some children came out into the garden. They had brought bread with them to feed the swans. The youngest child shouted, "Look, there's a new one!" All the children joyfully clapped their hands, and they ran to tell their parents.

Cake and bread were cast on the water for the swans. Everyone agreed that the new swan was the most beautiful of them all. The older swans bowed toward him.

He felt so shy that he hid his head beneath his wing. He was too happy, but not proud, for a kind heart can never be proud. He thought of the time when he had been mocked and persecuted. And now everyone said that he was the most beautiful of the most beautiful birds. And the lilac bushes stretched their branches right down to the water for him. The sun shone so warm and brightly. He ruffled his feathers and raised his slender neck, while out of the joy in his heart, he thought, "Such happiness I did not dream of when I was the ugly duckling."

Different from the Others

Surrendered Expectations
+ Forgiveness = Acceptance

> *At last the big egg cracked too. "Peep . . . Peep," said the*
> *young one, and tumbled out. He was big and very ugly.*
> *The mother duck looked at him. "He's awfully big for his*
> *age," she said. "He doesn't look like any of the others."*

"Sometimes I wonder if they got the babies in the nursery
mixed up," Marlene groaned in reference to her daughter,
Kari, who was causing trouble again. "I mean, I have four kids
and none of the others has even come close to causing us the
problems Kari has. We've raised her the same as the others."

"I saw that on Oprah once," Sarah said. "They interviewed
these mothers who got the wrong babies in the hospital. It was
awful."

I felt sick. My stomach hurt. I glanced at my friend, Patti,
across the table, and picked at my baked potato. I was no
longer hungry. Patti's expression was empathetic. It com-
forted me a little.

"She ran away again last week, as if that will help anything.
She was back within twenty-four hours. We didn't even bother
to call the police this time. I don't know what's wrong with

her. She does OK for a while and then it all starts up again, only worse. We've tried talking, grounding, taking away privileges—nothing works."

Have you tried listening? I wanted to ask. *Caring about her feelings? Accepting her where she is?* But I couldn't say anything without giving myself away. I was struggling with every problem Kari had and more. I knew what I needed, but I could never ask for it. Too often I would only get in touch with my needs during a conversation like this, where the discussion revolved around someone else who was a "problem" that people didn't quite know how to handle, and whom they really wished would just disappear.

I sensed the resignation in Marlene's voice—"We didn't even bother to call the police this time." She was giving up. "I hate to say this, but sometimes when she runs away, I find myself hoping she won't find her way back home again."

Tears welled up, but more in the area of my heart than in my eyes. Kari was not *"like any of the others."* An ugly duckling in her home, she stood alone. I identified with her—and hurt. I have always identified with the ugly duckling, feeling that I didn't quite fit in with the others in the henyard. Or anywhere else.

Over the years, I have met many other people who felt the same way. People like Kari. For anyone who feels "different" from the others, the story of the ugly duckling rings true.

When the ugly duckling tumbled out of his egg, I'm sure he wasn't immediately aware of his bigness and ugliness. But it wasn't long until the other ducks gathered around, making sure he became aware.

At times, when my life has flown out of control, I have felt like the ugly duckling as I have come under harsh judgment from those who just didn't understand why this particular bird couldn't "get it together." At other times, judgment has come in the form of ridicule for my behavior or views.

However, the pain of these experiences has also caused me to become aware of the pain I have caused in others. I realize that I, too, have judged and ridiculed.

Early in our marriage, my ex-husband let me know in no uncertain terms that there was one correct view of God—his, of course. So he talked and I listened. I got it down, then proceeded to judge and ridicule anyone who believed differently. I knew by heart the scriptures that supported our particular beliefs, so I just quoted them and let the Bible speak for itself. It was all a neat and tidy little faith walk.

Then my marriage disintegrated and the pain began. My neat little belief system began to unravel, and I realized I didn't have all the answers after all.

My growing awareness of my own unrealistic or unreasonable expectations of others to be or to do what I need is bringing about an increased tolerance inside of me. As I have faced unfulfilled expectations again and again, I have realized that I can deal with them in one of two ways: by allowing disillusionment to harden me, or by forgiving those who are incapable of offering the acceptance I need. I can forgive, sometimes confront, and then choose to continue to accept others, whether or not I myself feel accepted.

Author Max Lucado blends it all together in his book *No Wonder They Call Him the Savior:*

> It was Christ on the cross who taught us how to use expectations. Does he demand a lot? You better believe it. Does he expect too much? Only our best. Does he have expectations? Just that we leave everything, deny all, and follow him.
>
> Jesus couched his expectations with two important companions. Forgiveness and acceptance.
>
> One step behind the expectations of Christ come his forgiveness and tenderness. Tumble off the tightrope of what our Master expects and you land safely in his net of tolerance.[1]

There they are: expectations, forgiveness, acceptance, tolerance. This is the stuff daily life is made of. It makes or breaks our relationships with others and with God, and it definitely affects our self-perceptions.

What are our expectations in life? Are they realistic or unrealistic? How much are we able to forgive ourselves, God, and others? Can we walk in acceptance of who and what we can't change?

Expectations

"I wake up every morning and forgive everyone who will hurt me that day," I once heard a woman say. "It keeps me from unrealistically expecting that everyone will treat me kindly and having to face so much disappointment."

That sounds a bit pessimistic, but I've been trying it with one of my teenagers, and it's helping. On the other hand, is kindness really too much to expect, especially from those closest to us? Sometimes.

An expectation is an anticipation of something about to happen. The ugly duckling definitely failed to meet everyone's expectations. He was not like any of the others and, conformists that they were, the other ducks couldn't tolerate his differentness. They bit him, pecked at him, and kicked him. The most aristocratic fowl in the henyard even told the duckling's mother, *"I wish you could make him over again."*

Do we dare look back on our childhood and remember the times when an authority figure—a teacher, an aunt, or a grandparent—subtly or overtly communicated the same message to us?

Tragically, even the duckling's mother, the only one who had protected and defended him, seemed to have tired of dealing with his ugliness. She told him, *"I wish you were far away."*

If we never deal with our own unfulfilled expectations, we may find ourselves speaking the same horribly rejecting words to each other. My mother had expectations for my life. We never discussed them before she died, but I knew that, in her eyes, I hadn't:

- married the right man;
- gone to college as she'd hoped I would;
- settled and raised a family in the right city; or

- done anything significant with my life that she could feel proud of.

Sometimes I wondered if she wished I were *"far away."* And now I struggle with my expectations for my own kids. Expectations—fulfilled and unfulfilled, realistic and unrealistic—are a part of life.

You expect your spouse to be home for dinner unless informing you otherwise. You expect your next-door neighbors to keep their dog in their yard. You expect your car to have as much gas in it as it did the last time you drove it (even though your teenager has driven it since).

On a larger, more meaningful scale, you expect your spouse to love you "until death do us part." You expect your best friend to be loyal and not to gossip about you. You expect your parents to respect you as the adult you now are.

Expectations like these are normal (but not necessarily realistic). They cause us no problems until someone fails to live up to our standards and we smash into a wall of disappointment. Without exercising constant and ongoing forgiveness and acceptance, our world becomes as chaotic as the henyard as we flap our wings, kicking and screaming at those who disappoint us.

The answer is not to rid ourselves of expectations. That's impossible anyway, for many of them are on an unconscious level. And we do need to expect the best of others. Expectations can motivate positive growth in ourselves and in other people—if we can learn to discern healthy expectations from unhealthy ones. When someone expects (but doesn't demand) the best from me, I want to rise to meet those expectations. But if I fail, I deeply appreciate forgiveness and acceptance, even if I never change.

If the answer is not to rid ourselves of all expectations, then what? Here's what I try to keep in mind as I deal with expectations in my life:

(1) Expectations are the easiest to handle when they're on a

conscious level. As much as possible, I bring my expectations to the surface and acknowledge them.

(2) Keep expectations realistic. My unfulfilled expectations are as much my problem as anyone else's. People are human and will undoubtedly fail me for that reason alone. If I perceive that God has "failed" me, how realistic am I being? Unrealistic expectations can and must be surrendered.

(3) Anger—the human, sinful kind—is a sure sign that my expectations have turned into demands. Demands are sinful. Do I want to have to meet others' constant demands? Will they want to meet mine?

A few years ago, when I was still married, I finally acknowledged the intense loneliness I had endured on a daily basis, even while surrounded by five kids. Then I met a new friend, Peggy. I really liked her and wanted to get to know her better. She seemed to like me, too. I was sure we'd become fast friends.

But when I called, she would say, "Oh, I'd love to get together, but I'm taking Jenny to the doctor."

Or when I asked, she would say, "I'd really planned on going to Bible Study, but I'm so tired tonight."

Whenever I saw Peggy at church functions, she went out of her way to reach out to me—just like she did with everyone. Everyone liked Peggy, and everyone wanted a piece of her time.

Without warning, I found myself angry with her. I started to ignore her. Like a child, I wanted to punish Peggy for not spending more time with me. My expectations had turned into demands, and when she couldn't meet them, my disappointment turned into resentment.

If she picked up on the resentment, I would lose the friendship completely. But I had learned. I repented and began to accept Peggy for who she was—a dear friend who led a very *busy* life. After that I began to appreciate the time I did have with her.

If we look in the Bible, we can find places where unfulfilled expectations caused people great grief. The disciples had expectations of Jesus. Each expected to be the one to sit beside him in heaven (Mark 10:35–40); they expected him to set up his kingdom on earth (Luke 19:11); they had an urgent expectation for him to calm the storm on the Sea of Galilee (Luke 8:22–25). The disciples had many other expectations, some of which Jesus fulfilled and some of which he didn't.

Jesus had expectations of people, too. Take Peter, for example. Jesus expected Simon Peter's faith to be strong and not fail, strong enough that he might strengthen others. Jesus even told him that he had prayed for that to happen (Luke 22:31–32). Yet Peter, "the rock," failed Jesus miserably.

What happened when Jesus' expectations were not fulfilled? We have every indication that after his resurrection, Jesus *totally forgave* Peter. When the women showed up at the tomb to anoint Jesus' body (which was no longer there), the angel instructed them to "go, tell his disciples *and Peter,* 'He is going ahead of you into Galilee. There you will see him, just as he told you' " (Mark 16:7). Later Jesus told Peter to "Take care of my sheep" (John 21:16). The Lord could only trust Peter to do that if he had accepted him *as he was:* a very imperfect man, but a committed follower of the truth.

Forgiveness

Back in the henyard, the other ducks couldn't forgive the duckling for being different. Was he really even ugly, or was it that his differentness made him ugly to the others? After all, he was not like any of the others. He had shamed the entire henyard simply by showing up.

We all need forgiveness for our "ugliness" or differentness. People have both realistic and unrealistic expectations of us, and we need to have them forgive us for not living up to those expectations. Likewise, others need *our* forgiveness. But instead of forgiving others for their ugly or different parts, we too often try to get them to change so that we will no longer be embarrassed or inconvenienced by their ugliness.

To offer true forgiveness is to consistently lay down expectations and accept others, whether or not they ever move past their ugly duckling selves.

Volumes have been written and published on the subject of forgiveness. Yet we understand so little about how it really works and the tremendous privilege we have in both receiving and giving it.

Without forgiveness, couples separate, never to reconcile.

Without forgiveness, kids leave home, never to reconcile.

Without forgiveness, friends wound each other, never to reconcile.

Without forgiveness, churches split apart angrily, never to reconcile.

Without forgiveness, the distance between God and human beings widens.

Without forgiveness, our expectations sabotage relationships and we short-circuit the path to acceptance. If our goal is to live a life-style of acceptance, then forgiveness is often a daily must.

A friend of mine, Sue, couldn't stand smokers. They repulsed and disgusted her. She might be drawn to someone and even enter into a relationship with that person. Yet the minute she discovered that her new friend was a smoker, she was so turned off that she was unable to relate to the person at all. She hated this in herself and truly wanted to accept smokers. But she didn't know how.

"Sue, were you ever hurt by someone who smoked?" I gently prodded one day. "Your parents, maybe? Another relative?"

She looked thoughtful. "No, my parents didn't smoke." Then she tensed up. "But I had this babysitter when I was about ten—"

The tale that unfolded was one of sexual abuse by a teenage

babysitter, abuse that included the deliberate burning of a ten-year-old with cigarettes.

As Sue works through the forgiveness process, she will begin to accept smokers as fellow human beings, just as much in need of love and healing as she is. Through therapy, she is now doing that. Without forgiveness, Sue would remain trapped in the bondages of her childhood—the place where so many bondages start.

This is the importance that Chuck Swindoll places on forgiveness:

> You say you want to be different? You want to risk being innovative? You really desire to break free from your pharisaical ways but don't know where to begin? Start here. I don't know of anything more consuming, more constraining, than refusing to forgive. People who truly give their hearts are those who readily forgive their offenders. Go ahead and do the hard thing.
> . . . There's no better place to begin than with forgiveness. This single truth will break the inertia and unlock your prison, freeing you to fulfill your quest for character.[2]

"Huh. Easy for you to talk about," I hear you saying. "You have no idea what I've been through with so-and-so." Your own personal ugly duckling challenge, right?

Just for the record, I have my own so-and-sos. I can think of a couple of people I may have to spend the rest of my life forgiving if I want to have any personal peace. Easy? No.

No one ever said forgiveness was easy. My friend Sue, for example, deals often with the recurring memories of the abuse she received from her babysitter. Emotionally, she grieves deeply over the pain of losing her innocence at such a young age. She tells herself the truth, that she's worth more than that, that she never deserved abuse. Then she lets God touch those wounded places and heal them.

No, forgiveness is not a 1–2–3 formula. Not at all. As a matter of fact, I don't make my kids say, "I'm sorry, I forgive you" anymore unless we've "gutted it through" first—talked it over to a point where I know they mean it from deep down.

Unfortunately, for adults, the "gutting it through" process can take years. So—how badly do we want to be people who accept others? How badly do we want to fulfill the two great commandments, to love God above all else and to love others as we love ourselves? How badly do we want to risk everything and make the henyard a safe place for the ugly duckling? Jesus, bloody and beaten, his aching body nailed to a cross, spoke these words: "Father, forgive them, for they do not know what they are doing" (Luke 23:34). Can we say the same?

Acceptance

An ear-piercing, gut-wrenching wail rose from downstairs in the family room. At first I thought my teenage sons were just horsing around. I didn't move. But it continued—a mournful sound, a sobbing that tore at my heart. I jumped up and hurried down the stairs into the family room, where I found my oldest son, Travis, on the couch staring at the television. The cries came from Dwight's bedroom. I threw the door open to find my fourteen-year-old sitting on his bed, his head in his hands, his body shaking.

Dwight *never* cried.

"I hate him, I hate him, I hate him!"

"Travis?"

Dwight nodded. "I hate him."

"What did he do?"

"I hate him—I hate him!"

Stirred into near panic, I returned to the family room. "What did you do to him?" I shrieked at Travis.

Completely unmoved, Travis reluctantly pulled his eyes away from the television and eyed me warily. "Huh? Dwight?" He shrugged. "I don't know what he's so upset about. I just jiggled his skateboard a little. Like this." He got up and demonstrated. "He freaked out."

I motioned for Travis to follow me, and together we entered Dwight's room. Whimpering now, Dwight refused to look at either of us.

"What is it, Dwight?" I asked.

"I was—I was just working on my skateboard," he stammered. "He—it was the look on his face and—he—he's always putting me down. Why can't he leave me alone?" He finally looked up, his eyes pleading with his older brother. "Why can't he just like me the way I am?"

I turned to Travis and realized, as I looked at his set jaw, that he had the more serious problem.

"I can't stand skaters," he stated flatly.

Later in private, he told me, "I'm embarrassed. He's my brother, after all. He's a reflection on me. Look at his hair, his clothes, the way he talks, acts. It's disgusting."

Travis *expected* Dwight to be something other than a skater. Dwight *expected* Travis to accept him for who he was. Travis couldn't (or refused to) *forgive* Dwight for being a skater. Dwight couldn't (or refused to) *forgive* Travis for putting him down, for his nonacceptance. Travis would not *accept* Dwight where he was, if he never changed. Dwight, the rejected ugly duckling, put up his own wall of nonacceptance to ward off Travis's judgmental blows.

Nonacceptance threatened to split our family down the middle. It happens all the time in hundreds of thousands of homes, schools, businesses, and churches. Most nonaccepting attitudes are less overt than Travis's and Dwight's. Sometimes people's nonaccepting feelings simmer under the surface until one or both or a group of people explode over a surface issue that usually has little to do with the real issue that caused the nonacceptance in the first place. Family relationships are severed, friendships are cut off, and employees are kicked out—all over issues of nonacceptance.

Fortunately for us, this was a turning point in my sons' relationship with each other. As far as I know, they never talked about it again, but Travis began to respond to Dwight instead of reacting to him. Oh, the banter and teasing continued, but it was done now more in good-natured fun than with the old critical, bitter edge. I was proud of my boys.

I once saw a newspaper photograph that showed an orange-haired eighteen-year-old, wearing dozens of bracelets up each arm, a miniskirt, and a black leather jacket. The article below the photo reported:

> She began dressing in black leather and looking wild in high school as a way to find acceptance.
> "I liked the attention. This is all a stage and we were all just trying to outlook each other. You wouldn't be noticed or accepted until you looked real outrageous." [3]

The spike-haired punker you saw last week at the bus stop? He is in need of love and acceptance, just like you. Is he making a statement? Testing you? Asking, "Can you accept me when I look so different from you?"

What about the militant who caused a disturbance at last week's local political luncheon? The obnoxious preacher on the street corner condemning everyone to hell? The compulsive gossip across the street? Each is a person in need of God's love and acceptance—even if they don't recognize it themselves.

Jesus understands what it means to be treated like an ugly duckling. Utterly sinless, utterly acceptable, he "came to that which was his own, but his own did not receive him" (John 1:11). In his humanity, this must have caused Jesus great grief. In his divinity, he knew who he was, and was absolutely convinced of his acceptance by his Father.

We aren't so convinced of that. We need lots of help to believe it.

> Love, God's love, is radically other-centered. The great Russian novelist Dostoevski once wrote, "To love a person means to see a person as God intended him to be." That is a beautiful insight, but it does not go quite far enough. To love a person is not only to see a person in that way, but to act so that he will become the person God intends him to be. [4]

Can it be that when I confront my own ugly duckling self, I might then be able to confront yours? As I watch God pull the swan out in me, am I then able to help you discover the swan that God intends you to be? If this is truly what I want for you — if I really want to help you discover your swan, I can do three things:

- I can look honestly at myself and admit my own weaknesses and sins. In my swan process, I am at times both an ugly duckling and a judgmental, self-righteous, aristocratic fowl.
- I can give up my right to control you or to tell you how to live your life.
- I can move toward you in God's love, stopping my own ugly duckling from running and my judgmental self from expecting more of you than you're capable of in your swan process.

Can any of us do it? Can we move beyond the ugly ducklings in each other and discover the secret of the swan on the other side? As the newborn ducks found out, it's a big world out there. In one still, small corner, "Peep, peep!" An ugly duckling is born. A swan? No way. Well, maybe —

Go ahead. Give it a try. What a wonderful privilege to play such an important role in God's big plan for his big world. To take an ugly duckling who is *"not like any of the others"* and free the swan inside!

"How Big the World Is!"

Understanding the Swan Process and Its Power

"How big the world is!" piped the little ones, for they had much more space to move around in now than they had had inside the egg.

"Do you think that this is the whole world?" quacked their mother. "The world is much larger than this. It stretches as far as the minister's wheat fields, though I have not been there . . . .

It is definitely a big world, much bigger than most of us allow ourselves to experience. We're afraid to venture out of the henyard, afraid of who and what we might encounter.

Oh, there's plenty to do inside the henyard; strutting around and taking charge like the aristocratic fowl, nurturing all the little ducklings like the mother duck, or biting and pecking the other ducks who get in our way. These seem to be quite noble and important tasks, keeping us busy for perhaps our whole lives. And when the ugly duckling runs away from the henyard for sheer survival's sake, we cluck our tongues and say, "That poor ugly duckling is rebelling. Eventually he'll come to his senses and return to the fold." We stick to business as usual. After all, life in the henyard must go on.

Meanwhile, out in the big, wide world, the ugly duckling is

becoming a beautiful swan. Painfully. Outside the "safety" of the henyard he has to go through untold miseries.

Now the ugly duckling didn't necessarily know that there was even a swan to become. He probably wasn't conscious of the process. And he was unaware of the reflection that awaited him on the surface of the pond.

Nonetheless, conscious or not, it was happening—because God is the creator of new life. The swan was new life for the duckling. Miserable beyond belief, he thought he wanted to die. But he misinterpreted his suffering, as we all do. Out of great suffering, swans are born.

Not too many ducklings are willing to suffer enough to reach their swans. I happen to believe that Jesus' story of the wedding banquet (Matt. 22:1–14) is not about salvation but is about the abundant life God promises to every one of his kids. "For many are invited, but few are chosen" (v. 14).

Our reflection in the pond is our door into the wedding banquet. The swan is our wedding garment, the one required if we are to participate in the banquet.

We know our swan is near when:

(1) we are able to embrace our suffering;

(2) we are able to repent of unloving behavior and receive God's forgiveness without feeling that our sin has anything to do with our value;

(3) we make growing in love for God, others, and ourselves our highest goal in life.

Acceptance of the process, our own and one another's, is vital; we have to let it happen. We ugly ducklings may be unconscious of the swan process, but we are very aware of our need for acceptance.

The need for acceptance—whether we stay in the henyard or run into the big world—is so crucial and deep that some of us will do anything to find it: take drugs, join cults, marry abusers. I once bought an expensive jacket to gain acceptance from the friend who was shopping with me. In the past, I have acquired unhealthy vices for the same reason.

Acceptance has a power all of its own. Why? What exactly is acceptance? Once we understand what acceptance is, we will understand our desperate craving for it, see why the lack of it can be so devastating, know why withholding it from others is so damaging, and see why our ability to offer it unconditionally can bring such healing.

A few years ago I was forced to find my identity outside of my relationship with my husband. A strong and forceful man, his reputation and image preceded us and I followed in his shadow. Others' acceptance of me was determined first by their acceptance of him.

But when he was gone and I had no more buffers, I felt raw pain when other ducks in the henyard pecked and bit me. In pain, I stepped outside the henyard. They didn't try to coax me back. And I began to experience the world in its largeness. Outside of the boundaries of the henyard, I didn't know how to act. As miserable as I was in the henyard, at least I knew what was expected of me. I am so grateful that God sets up his home in human hearts, not inside or outside of henyards.

When I was outside the henyard I began to discover my swan. Many have told me it shouldn't have happened that way. It should have happened inside the henyard. Maybe. I don't know, and it no longer matters.

The important thing is that someone took the risk, someone left the henyard to find me, someone thought I was worth it. It only takes one or two.

And it doesn't have to be Mother Teresa. Or Martin Luther King, Jr. Or Billy Graham. Anyone can take the risk. It can be me, or you, or both of us together.

Acceptance is allowing God to enlarge our world by reaching outside the henyard. Acceptance is the ability to receive the ugly ducklings of the world warmly and unconditionally, without reservation, no matter who they are, what they've done, or how they look. Acceptance is caring enough to risk getting dirty. Acceptance is giving others the freedom to be who they are. Acceptance is letting God bring the swan out of ugly ducklings. Ultimately, acceptance is surrendering your expectations, risking forgiveness, and loving others the way Jesus does.

Who could teach us about acceptance better than Jesus? His is the only kind of acceptance worth our pursuit, the only kind of acceptance that heals without qualification.

Is it possible to accept ourselves and others as Jesus does? Are we talking about something that is impossible to attain? Are we setting ourselves up for failure?

Romans 15:7 says, "Accept one another, then, just as Christ accepted you." I have always believed that God wouldn't set us up for failure. Why would God ask us to do what he knew we couldn't do? As we consider acceptance, then, exactly what does God require of us? How does Christ accept us?

Acceptance is not a passive position that we maintain as others move toward us. Acceptance is an assertive action that happens as we move toward others. It's taking the world's humanity deep inside of us and making a commitment to stay, whatever may come. It's giving up our expectations and often sacrificing our reputations. It's constant and ongoing forgiveness, resulting in a tolerance that transcends our humanity. It's believing in the ugly duckling and trusting the swan process, no matter what the other ducks say or think. It's loving beyond our fear of the unveiling of another. To decide to accept others unconditionally may be the greatest risk you will ever take, because you have to give up so much of who you are.

I recently watched an interview with Walter Anderson, editor of *Parade* magazine, on a local Seattle talk show. The interviewer questioned Anderson about his book, *The Greatest Risk of All*. After the author expounded for some time on certain successful people and the risks they faced as they moved toward their success, the interviewer turned to him and asked, "Walter, what is the greatest risk of all?"

Anderson quickly answered, "Vulnerability."

Raised by an alcoholic, abusive father, Walter Anderson eventually quit high school at sixteen and left home in order to survive. Many others in his situation would have moved toward bitterness and cynicism—and justifiably so, since the wounds pierced deep. Yet he made the choice to stay vulnerable, and in doing so, achieved success.

Vulnerability. Acceptance. Do they go hand in hand? Can you have one without the other? You can only accept and be accepted by the others in your life as you make yourself vulnerable to them.

Without vulnerability, we relate to one another's shells. I suppose that is a place to start, for if in our relationships we can accept the outer shell, we can risk the next step—offering more vulnerable parts of ourselves so that we can provide acceptance of a deeper kind and at a deeper level.

I remember times when fear of rejection paralyzed any kind of vulnerability I might ever have expressed. God finally showed me that in withholding my inner self from others, I was sinning, refusing to relate on more than just a superficial level. At that point I decided I wanted to be a vulnerable person because I knew it was what God wanted, whether or not acceptance followed.

So I became deliberately vulnerable—even in situations that I knew to be emotionally unsafe. Sometimes acceptance followed, and sometimes it didn't. But I was no longer afraid of rejection. I had faced it and lived.

Reaching Toward

Sometimes our individual weaknesses make us feel unworthy of the love and acceptance of God and others. This feeling paralyzes our ability to reach toward others for what we need. But *your* reluctance to be vulnerable does not give *me* permission to love you less. Because you are so conscious of your ugly duckling self, and unable to make choices, the ball is in my court. But I can't hit a ball that I can't see. If you won't let me know what you need, how can I reach toward you?

I once worked with a woman who, on the surface, appeared

confident, self-assured, together—in need of nothing and no one. In a rare moment of vulnerability, I discovered something different. I watched her almost crumble as we talked one day about her life. Almost.

Sensing her need, I pushed. "Can I hug you?" I asked and moved a step toward her.

"No." She shook her head firmly.

Ouch, I thought, feeling the pain of rejection. The wall came back up. The moment passed and our conversation was over.

This happened on a Friday. All weekend I struggled. Had I misinterpreted her need? I was sure she had communicated a nonverbal need for a hug. I was hurt by her rebuff, and I thought about closing myself off to her.

Monday morning I found her note on my desk.

"Thanks for reaching out to me. It's one of the things I love about you. I'm sorry for my reaction. It's my problem—don't give up."

This ugly duckling, my coworker, had suffered severe pecking and biting at the hands of others. I gladly gave her the time she needed, and I let her know that I would always be there to help bring out as much of her swan as she would allow.

Unconditional acceptance is not based on a person's ability to communicate needs. It is something we give freely, whether or not the other person feels worthy of it or is able to ask for it. Unlike respect or trust, acceptance is not something we make others earn. We offer acceptance because we know our own desperate need for it in the light of our own sin, and because God loves and accepts us as we are. Can we do any less for one another?

But why is it often so difficult or seemingly impossible to reach toward others who are in need of our acceptance? And why does so much of our reaching toward others involve pecking and biting?

I have grown in accepting others as a result of getting in touch with my own shortcomings as contrasted with God's holiness, but I trip up when confronted with legalistic, rigid forms of Christianity. Because of my many years as a full-fledged and self-righteous, aristocratic fowl (and my paralyzing fear of ending up there once again), I find it extremely difficult to reach out toward ugly ducklings who have this particular mind-set. We all have our areas. Your stumbling block may be the media or "secular humanists," Catholics or Pentecostals, your "perfect" sister or your workaholic father.

I remember my horror one time when I discovered a particular sin in my life, and also the outstretched arms of a friend who drew me close "as if I were an angel of God, as if I were Christ Jesus himself" (Gal. 4:14). If my friend had recoiled from me in like horror, I wonder if I would ever have let anyone draw me close again.

How difficult will it be for us to disentangle our arms from across our chests? How many hurting people—some of them those we love the most—will have to withdraw from us in anger or disillusionment? What will it take?

Let's start with trust; trust in an almighty God, the one who accepts us unequivocally. Jesus accepted the woman at the well who had been married five times (John 4:7–26). He accepted Zacchaeus, the hated chief tax collector (Luke 19:1–10). Jesus even accepted Paul, a once legalistic, self-righteous Pharisee (Phil. 3:4–6).

If God, in sinless Jesus, can reach out, drawing us close, then we too can reach out—to all kinds of ugly ducklings in this big world, no matter where they are in their process of becoming swans.

Taking In

When we accept, we take in. Paul exhorted the Romans to "accept (*proslambánō*) one another." He was asking them to receive or accept one another in their homes or circle of acquaintances.[1] The literal meaning of that Greek word is to take to oneself. To me, this "taking in" means to embrace, bring close, and love deeply.

It's up for interpretation whether I was kicked out of the henyard or left of my own accord. It was probably a combination of the two. All I know is that I desperately needed to be taken in, but I gave opposite signals to those who might have wanted to do this: "I'm fine. I can take care of myself. No problem. I don't need you or anyone else. Leave me alone. Life stinks."

Who would *want* to take me in? My internalized pain had made me self-protective and even mean at times. And I was growing meaner by the minute as I added to my hurts.

Yet deep inside, I longed for someone to take me in, to look past the meanness, my ugly duckling, and to help me release my swan.

Did I blame them? Not at all. I don't usually feel like taking in people like me, either. Besides, can't we be selective in who we take to ourselves? We aren't expected to accept everyone, are we? What about the pedophile? Or the fallen TV evangelist? Or the punk rocker? C'mon, get real. God doesn't expect us to "take in" the drunk driver who killed the small child? Especially if that small child was mine?

But Paul didn't qualify it. He just said, "Accept one another."

"Forget it," you may say. "I can't do that. It's too hard."

I agree. It's too hard. I remember the time a chubby, six-year-old girl rode her bike over my three-year-old son's leg, snapping it in two. The little girl left him sobbing on the driveway, where I found him a few moments later. The mother and father never did appear and never spoke to anyone in our family again, even though they lived next door and had been friendly until then. You mean I'm supposed to accept, "take in," people like that? I'm supposed to open up, making myself vulnerable once again?

John Fischer, in his disturbing book *Real Christians Don't Dance*, talks about God's kind of spontaneous dance, "whenever life spills out on the floor." He goes on to say:

Most people, even those who pride themselves in their dancing, are afraid of this spontaneous dance. They're afraid of anything they can't control; and His dance is wild, unmanageable, even mad. But most important, it's vulnerable, open to criticism—the quality they fear most.[2]

There's that word again—*vulnerable*. We can't take anyone in unless we open something up—our hearts. And fear of vulnerability locks us up tight. In our swan process, afraid of attack, pain, or hurt, we long to return to the self-protective egg from which we were hatched.

But it's cold and lonely inside the egg! I know. And once we have risked vulnerability and pecked our way out, once we have entered into the swan process in the big world, there is really no returning to the egg.

Vulnerability—the greatest risk of all. God's dance is vulnerable; is ours?

Standing Firm

True acceptance doesn't waver. It's a commitment that goes beyond today and far into tomorrow. True acceptance is the refusal to budge from someone's life, no matter how often the lights go out, the welcome mat is snatched away, and you bump up against walls in the dark.

What will keep us standing firm when we are pushed to the absolute max of our tolerance level? How can we accept again and again and again—when someone comes up and says, "I blew it again," and we want to scream in frustration and anger? That's when we tap into Jesus' energy, always available to us, and forgive the seven times seventieth time. We walk the precarious edge of believing the best of the person, yet understanding humanness, we are fully aware that another "again" could be just around the corner.

In the middle of a serious spiritual thrashing and flailing, as I tried to find my way out of the maze of pain that now directed my life, I made a hundred mistakes a day. Or so it

seemed. I couldn't get anything under control, and some days
I didn't care enough to try. But I had a couple of friends who
spoke two important words to me over and over and over
again: "It's OK." Then they just sat with me, caressed my
feathers, and fed me bread. They were always there, always
loving, always caring, always accepting, no matter what. They
believed in me when I didn't believe in myself. They confronted me gently, carefully. They didn't push, just encour-
aged me to keep moving—when I was ready.

At times, when it looked like I wouldn't make it, they grieved.
But they never surrendered their position of acceptance. They
stayed—and stayed—and stayed. They stood firm. They're still
here now, the kind of friends I want around for life.

Loving Beyond

God's kind of acceptance transcends anything we might do
or be in any one moment. It doesn't depend on where we are
or who we're with.

Jesus made a significant point when he told us to turn the
left cheek when someone has already punched our right, to
hand over our jacket when someone has already ripped off our
shirt, and to offer to go two miles with someone who has already forced us to go one (Matt: 5:39–41).

Now I'm not an advocate of standing still and taking abuse.
However, every once in a while I will turn the other cheek,
especially with my kids, to make a statement or to teach them
a certain truth. Jesus is telling us that we can choose to place
ourselves in a sacrificial position for the sake of the gospel, for
a higher purpose. Like he did.

Why not? Why not enlarge our world beyond the compo-
nents of a quota system in our churches? Why not throw our
church doors wide open and invite the people we most look
down our noses at? What about the gay community, members
of the local humanist organization, or the Jewish community?
Dare we invite them in? Not that they would come. Our self-

righteous escapades and public scandals of recent years have caused them to be as afraid of Christianity as Christians are of them.

Acceptance of others often involves the sacrifice of things we hold dear—our reputations, our need for approval, and our security, to name a few. In certain situations, when we withhold judgment and choose to accept, we risk being misunderstood and perhaps judged ourselves.

It happened to Jesus. The self-righteous Pharisees wanted to know why he hung out with tax collectors and "sinners." Jesus replied in his simple way: "It is not the healthy who need a doctor, but the sick" (Matt. 9:10–12). We are all among the sick. And Jesus isn't ashamed to be seen with us, to hang around with us, to accept us right where we are—in our sin.

Judas Iscariot was not only a sinner (like the other eleven disciples), but also a traitor. How did Jesus respond to him? He washed his feet. Jesus didn't wait until Judas left the upper room so that he could avoid washing his feet.

> *The evening meal was being served, and the devil had already prompted Judas Iscariot, son of Simon, to betray Jesus . . . . When he had finished washing their feet, he put on his clothes and returned to his place. . . . As soon as Judas had taken the bread, he went out. And it was night (John 13:2, 12, 30).*

What was Jesus thinking as he knelt before his betrayer and took the disciple's sandy feet tenderly into his hands? How Jesus' heart must have ached as he anticipated what his companion was about to do.

Jesus moved far beyond tolerance. He accepted Judas—before, during, and after betrayal. He called Judas "friend," even as the betrayal took place (Matt. 26:50).

Believing In

The mother duck believed in the ugly duckling—for no other reason than that he was (or at least appeared to be) her own child. How much we all need someone to believe the best about us, especially when we're not walking in a way that makes us worthy of that kind of trust in our character. That's what acceptance is in this sense. Loyalty to your friend doesn't mean you refuse to believe he or she is capable of a certain wrong behavior, but that you trust in that person's swan process. When all we are showing others, for whatever reason, is our ugly duckling selves, we need someone, somewhere, to keep believing that the swan is emerging.

We often rise (or sink) to whatever others expect (or accuse us of). I have been referred to as "rebellious" enough times that the word itself can bring out rebellious behavior in me. I recently received a "pacesetter's" award; someone believed in me and saw me not as rebellious but as a pacesetter. It's truly amazing what that award has done for my perception of myself. For now I see that much of my pacesetting behavior could be and is interpreted as rebellious. That's not to say I'm not rebellious at times, but who besides God can accurately judge the intentions and attitudes of my heart?

I need those who will not judge me by my external behavior, but will believe in the character of my heart, where gut issues originate, and where the swan process has begun. These people believe in the new person God is trying to create and nurture in me.

Sacrificing Self

I became romantically involved with a man named Jerry after my divorce. One night, in the middle of a passionate situation rapidly spinning out of control, Jerry made a sacrifice for me. We had discussed sex outside of marriage. Jerry's convictions were not as stringent as mine, but so far we had managed to keep things under control. Jerry had never pushed, though, and I couldn't quite figure it out. I was as programmed as most women to believe that single men were after only one thing.

"Would you make love to me if I asked you to?" I wondered aloud.

"No."

"*No?*" I echoed, surprised, and feeling slightly rejected. "Why not?"

"Because I know you. I know how you'd feel afterwards and I don't want to cause you that kind of pain."

Jerry, a hot-blooded American male, sacrificed his own sexual desires to accept me where he knew my heart really was, even though my emotions and body cried out something different. When we broke up, I was able to walk away with my dignity and self-respect intact, something that wouldn't have been possible had Jerry not made a sacrifice for me that night.

Risking For

Has anyone ever taken a risk for you? How did it feel? When someone is willing to suffer loss, damage, or injury for me, it means a lot.

When we accept each other unconditionally, we risk being misunderstood. People wondered about Jesus because of the people he hung around with. Certain people might wonder about you if you hung around with me—especially if I pulled one of the crazy shenanigans I've been known for in the past. Or if I boldly stated one of my typical, sweeping generalizations that constantly get me into trouble. Others might assume that you think the way I do. That's a risk you would take.

Unconditional acceptance carries the risk of the unknown. If we make the decision to accept each other without knowing everything, we may be in for some heavy-duty surprises as our personalities and life philosophies unfold. The more we accept each other, the more we will grow to trust each other, the more of ourselves we will share, and the more our world will expand. It can be scary because it's unfamiliar. Walter Anderson says,

Clearly, taking a risk is difficult—and danger is a vital part of risk-taking. To risk is to stretch further than we have before.[3]

In learning to accept, we don't just risk and stretch one time. We do it again and again and again. I do it for you, and you do it for me. We stretch for the people and places in our lives; for our families and for our friends. Acceptance is simply being a friend—a no-holds-barred, no-questions-asked, no-explanations-needed kind of friend. John Fischer talks about the accepting kind of friend that Jesus was (and is):

> *If Jesus didn't condemn the world, why should we?*
> *Jesus even earned the label "friend of sinners." This is truly remarkable when you consider that he was sinless. If anyone had the right to be "holier-than-thou," it was Christ; and if anyone should feel condemned around Him, it was sinners—especially sinners like prostitutes or crooked tax collectors. Yet these people found him to be their friend; a strong affirmation of Christ's humility as the Son of Man.*
> *It's time for Christians to rejoin the human race, to face our own humanity and find the ability to look compassionately on our other friends in the world. Our link with the world is our humanness. We don't have wings and we don't glow in the dark, but we know who forgives us and gives us hope.*[4]

The ugly duckling needs a friend. You do. I do, too. Jesus said, "Love each other as I have loved you. Greater love has no one than this, that one lay down his life for his friends" (John 15:12–13). The Son of man laid down his life. Now it's our turn. Through the power of acceptance, we can choose to lay down our lives and enlarge our world for our ugly duckling friends. The next step is to take the plunge into the water. Can we swim?

3

Splash! Into the Water

Enlarging Your Pond and Influencing Your World

> *The next day the weather was gloriously beautiful. The sun shone on the forest of burdock plants. The mother duck took her whole brood to the moat. "Quack . . . Quack . . . " she ordered.*
>
> *One after another, the little ducklings plunged into the water. For a moment their heads disappeared, but then they popped up again and the little ones floated like so many corks. Their legs knew what to do without being told. All of the new brood swam very nicely, even the ugly one.*

The only ducklings who make it to swan status are those who risk getting in the water. If the ugly one had stayed on shore, he would never have discovered the joy of swimming, and found out that he was actually good at it. Of course, maybe if he'd never gotten into the water, he'd never have entered the henyard and gotten hurt, either. Maybe he'd still be safe on the shore. Safe but alone.

When we watch our loved ones plunk into the water, we also have a choice: whether or not to urge them on. Whether to cheer safely from the shore, or to join them in their own discovery process.

What a risk! If we join them, we don't know where we'll

end up. It might be far from the comfort of our church, our Bible study, our own home. We might end up in the henyard, pecked at and bit simply for hanging out with an ugly duckling.

Choosing to accept and encourage the swan process in one another makes a huge difference in how we grow and how we relate—or *if* we grow and relate at all.

But it's important to count the cost before we join an ugly duckling in the pond—or honor our own swan process and jump in ourselves. It's important especially because we may never have been in the water before. Can we swim?

Yes, it's a risky venture. There's a lot at stake. Yet true acceptance of ourselves and others requires that we take the plunge, get into the water, and give it a try.

Bringing Healing

Acceptance was not a particular issue in my life until I found myself on the threshold of divorce after a marriage of thirteen years. Suddenly I was thrust into a situation where many people, especially many Christian people, seemed to be uncomfortable. The way I chose to cope—or not cope—with this situation made everyone even more uncomfortable, including me.

In a sense, my divorce was my shove into the water. Born an ugly duckling, I had never attempted to swim. I had never needed to. I had also managed to keep most of my ugly duckling self hidden. But it all began to emerge at the time of my divorce. I may have been swimming, but I was definitely aware of my differentness more than ever.

I know now that my divorce was not the issue. The divorce was not what made me an ugly duckling—it only helped the inherent ugliness of sin come to the surface.

Unfortunately, though, I began to focus on my divorce, causing others to focus on it, too. I began to condemn myself, and I internalized the condemnation of others who didn't understand. I wondered, *What is God thinking about all this?*

Caught in a vortex of confusing opinions on my unfortunate circumstances, I waited for something to happen. Either God would punish me with cancer or some other deadly malady, or God would express his acceptance of this divorcée through the body of Christ.

Neither happened—at least not right away.

I sometimes thought that illness might have been a blessing—less painful than some of the misery I endured during the next few months, much of which I caused myself.

I sensed that some people wanted to be accepting and supportive, but they didn't want anyone to think they "condoned" divorce, so in spite of their good intentions, they distanced themselves from me. They stayed on the shore.

In agony, I swam for my life. The breach widened, and we could no longer reach each other. Finally, so that I wouldn't feel the pain of rejection so acutely, I quit looking back at the shore. Any hope that those on the banks might follow me into the water had died.

"Who needs them?" I casually said over my shoulder as I began my long, treacherous, and lonely journey away from the body of Christ. I needed them, but there was no way I would admit it—not to myself or to anyone else. Not even to God.

The distancing on both sides short-circuited God's healing process, the redemptive work he wanted to do in my life. The sting of rejection (real or imagined, "deserved" or "undeserved") can quickly turn into the worst kind of gut-wrenching agony. Before we can see God's perspective, we're racing to be the first one to swim away from the other.

Dr. Larry Crabb calls this self-protection:

> . . . *everyone develops a style of relating designed to avoid the experience of deep personal pain—and that is the sin of self-protection.*
>
> . . . *[it] occurs when our legitimate thirst for receiving love creates a demand to not be hurt that overrides a commitment to lovingly involve ourself with others. When that demand for self-*

*protection interferes with our willingness to move toward others
with their well-being in view, then the law of love is violated.*[1]

Thinking we are protecting ourselves from those mean
ducklings whose one goal in life is to make us miserable, we
lock ourselves into the isolation and darkness of our own
souls. My soul, at this point in my life, was a dangerous place
for me to hide. What could have prevented this descent into its
deep, dark corridors?

Keith Miller, in his book *Sin, the Ultimate Deadly Addiction*,
reveals to us so clearly God's provision for our sin and the
healing that is available to us when the body of Christ is func-
tioning as God originally intended.

> *And the church evidently discovered that only when Christians
> kept facing squarely the specific behaviors their sin caused,
> repented, confessed them openly in the Christian community,
> asked for forgiveness, and made amends in every way possible
> could they receive the healing forgiveness they continued to need.
> Through this process, God kept washing the sins from people's
> minds, in the same way you would clean a blackboard.*
>
> *. . . The inner conflict was over, and forgiven Christians were
> acceptable to God, to their brothers and sisters in Christ, and to
> themselves. They didn't have to run compulsively from their sins
> and fear and pain. They had confessed them and received God's
> forgiveness and the love of the community. They were free to
> breathe deeply, to live and love again for another day.*[2]

What paved the way in the New Testament church for sinners like you and me to admit our sins, repent, confess our
sins, receive forgiveness, and make amends to those we hurt by
our sinful behavior? Acceptance.

Acceptance is crucial and absolutely necessary in the recovery process. We must experience acceptance of our ugliness,
rather than the disgust we've been used to, if we are ever to
transcend it. Once we have heard someone say, "Yeah, so
you're an ugly duckling. We all are. Let's focus on what we can
become—swans," then we can move into recovery. By recov-

ery, I mean the healing that we are forever in need of because of sin's destructive power.

Providing a Safe Place

A safe place provides us the freedom to swim the way God intended — to be ourselves, to confess our sins and weaknesses without fear of judgment, condemnation, or ridicule. It's a place where love covers, protects, and delivers.

One reason I couldn't grow in my marriage is that I didn't have such a place. Instead of coming alongside and offering to help me grow, my ex-husband would criticize me for not knowing enough Scripture.

I began to close up. If my marriage wasn't a safe place to make mistakes and grow from them, what was? Eventually I quit trying altogether.

The tragedy was that because I had God and my husband all mixed up together, I couldn't see God as a safe place, either.

But the truth is that God is always a safe place. Psalm 32:7 sums it up: "You are my hiding place; you will protect me from trouble and surround me with songs of deliverance." God was a safe place for King David, who wrote this psalm — a man who, by his own admission, was one of the worst sinners of all. God doesn't change. He is a safe place for us, too.

Many times it seems as if God is the only safe place we have. Yet God's ideal is that we function as his healing body and provide a safe place for one another as well. Because of God's Holy Spirit dwelling within us, the potential is there.

The key to providing a safe place for fellow sinners through our acceptance of them is illustrated in Jesus' parable of the Pharisee and the tax collector. The Pharisee thanked God that he wasn't a rotten sinner like so many others — "robbers, evildoers, adulterers — or even like this tax collector." The tax collector, on the other hand, wouldn't even raise his eyes to heaven, but beat his chest and said, "God, have mercy on me, a sinner" (Luke 18:9–14).

We cannot walk with others through their ugliness if we deny our own. It is only in the discovery of our own Pharisaism that we become a safe place for other sinners. Let's keep beating our chests and crying out for God's mercy.

People Are Acceptable

If it weren't so tragic, I would find it amusing how intolerant I can be of others when I am so desperately in need of acceptance myself, simply because I'm a person too.

I know the truth—ugly ducklings are acceptable—no matter where they are in their process of recognizing their swans. But I don't like it when they act dumb, nerdy, sneaky, weak, or all of the above. Just like you, I have a list of attributes that attract me to people and another list of sure turnoffs.

I remember having an especially difficult time with one woman's swan process. We worked together and sometimes she'd do the corniest things. I remember the day she went home from work, mad at everyone, and returned the next morning only to throw open the main door and scream, "Good morning, Vietnam!"

I pretended not to know her for the rest of the day.

Then there is the wimpy friend of mine who ran out of gas on the freeway. Instead of getting out of the car and walking to the nearest gas station, she sat in the car and prayed for her husband or someone to come by and rescue her. (I was the one who happened by. I was supposedly her answer to prayer, but I was still exasperated with her.)

Luci Swindoll says it well in her book *Alchemy of the Heart*:

> Let somebody in the local church show a crack in his or her life and what happens? Fellow church members are all over him, trying to straighten him out. Whatever it is that's on our "rejection list," we camp on that, outlining ways for certain people to behave so they will be acceptable to God. But what we are really saying is "so that they will be acceptable to us." [3]

How ludicrous for us to claim that our acceptability depends on our personal and current list of rights and wrongs, often not even determined by the Word of God, but by societal and cultural trends. While we stand on the shore, checking out each ugly duckling, wondering whether or not we can tolerate his or her flaws, the ducklings are looking smaller and smaller as they paddle away from us.

Our acceptability is determined by only one thing: "But now in Christ Jesus you who once were far away have been brought near through the *blood of Christ*" (Eph. 2:13). Later on, in this same letter to the Ephesians, Paul wrote that "In him and through faith in him we may approach God with freedom and confidence" (Eph. 3:12).

Does that sound like God is scrutinizing our behavior and life-style before deciding whether or not to accept us? Not at all. We find acceptance with God because of two things— Jesus' shed blood, and our faith in him. If God accepts us, can we do any less than accept one another?

Promoting Honesty

I remember being with a friend one day and wanting to tell her about my abusive marriage. Recently divorced, I needed someone to care about my trauma.

"He used the Bible as a hammer," I told her. (First step.)

"I'm so sorry. How awful."

"You know, the Bible actually kind of scares me now." (Second step.)

"I can understand why. It condemns you because of how you interpret it."

Safe so far. "I'm not reading the Bible now. I can't even go to church sometimes . . . ." (Third step.)

"It takes time to heal. Give yourself time."

Her loving response over time allowed me to be more and more honest. Inner healing followed.

When unconditional love and acceptance are the rule, we are able to bare our souls to one another, ugliness and all.

On the other hand, if you've had a history of baring your soul (fears, desires, sins, weaknesses, etc.) and being judged and punished as a result, it's unlikely you'll want to do it again.

I suppose I have become a bit of a cynic in this area. I'm careful these days what I share honestly with whom. Not because I have anything to hide, but because I've been misunderstood too many times. My friend mentioned above is the exception I have discovered. It's more rare than not when I meet a person who will withhold judgment and accept me at face value. Someone who will enjoy and appreciate this duckling's efforts to get into the water, refusing to analyze *why* I got into the water and where I'm swimming to.

Don't we all want our relationships to be honest? Do we really like having to hide certain areas of our lives from each other for fear of judgment, rejection, or punishment? The degree of honesty with which people will approach you is directly determined by the degree of acceptance you express.

Thanks to God's faithfulness in convicting us of our own sinful natures, we grow in our ability to accept others in their sinful natures. They, in turn, are able to continue to risk relating to us more and more honestly. We need each other.

Bonds

True acceptance tightly bonds us and creates a unit that is difficult to break once it is sealed. You would think our shared humanity, with its beginnings as ugly ducklings, would unite us and connect us to one another. Not necessarily—especially if the other ducklings around us seem to have their lives fairly well put together, and ours seem to be flying apart.

Certainly our shared bond in the body of Christ will help us shake the often uncomfortable feeling of separation and connect us again to the whole. Not always. We may begin to talk about our feelings, hoping for validation and acceptance, and receive instead a blank stare that communicates a number of things: "Get a grip." "It can't be that bad." "Look at all you've got to be thankful for."

Sometimes, when the pain is so great that we can't even discuss it, we begin to drift, choosing to isolate ourselves from a community that could bring healing. Who's at fault? Usually it's a joint effort. But until we accept and are accepted again, we drift further and further away from each other.

I sat across the table recently from the leader of an international ministry and confessed a major fear connected to my relationship with the Lord.

"It was awful, the utter terror that surfaced," I explained. "I know it's irrational . . . ." I began to feel stupid for even experiencing it, let alone telling her about it.

Being the spiritual person that Jane was, she could have said, "The Bible says, 'perfect love casts out fear.' You need to be made perfect in love." Or she could have said, "You've struggled with this for about five years now. Don't you think it's about time . . . ?" Since the problem called for a practical solution, she might have advised, "You have to face your fears, you know. Hang in there." All these things may have been true, and at some point I would need to hear them, to examine my fear rationally. But first the fear needed to be acknowledged and accepted for the feeling that it was.

I will forever be indebted to her, for that is exactly what she did. She didn't say anything right away. She listened and nodded, *accepting* my feeling. Then she took it a step further. By the pained expression on her face, I knew she felt my fear and *empathized* with me. She did one final thing. Her next words were: "You know, when I feel that kind of fear, I . . . ." She *identified*. And the bonding was complete. I will never again hesitate to talk with her about my fears.

Jesus prayed for us once: "May they be brought to complete unity to let the world know that you sent me and have loved them even as you have loved me" (John 17:23).

Our acceptance of each other brings the kind of unity that expresses Jesus' life and the Father's love to the world.

Bringing Praise to God

The second part of Paul's admonition to "Accept one an-other, then, just as Christ accepted you," gives us the reason: ". . . in order to bring praise to God" (Rom. 15:7). How does acceptance bring praise to God? Paul wrote this after a long exhortation in Romans 14 about judging one another. He dis-cussed different interpretations of sacred holy days, eating meat, and drinking wine. Can you imagine the mixed-up mess of teaching that circulated in New Testament times on the rights and wrongs of these insignificant external issues because of the diverse groups of people who were becoming followers of Christ?

We have a similar situation today. There are at least two ex-isting extremes on any issue, and at each extreme you will find a faithful group of Christians claiming they have a corner on the truth. And everyone can point to Scripture to support their favorite "truth." Our pet beliefs can be perfectly harmless until we start hammering them into others, obnoxiously insist-ing that they embrace our viewpoint. Of course, our beliefs do influence and inspire our feelings and actions, creating a life-style that may be different from our neighbor's and may cause great conflict. These conflicts are evident to all, and often make Christianity look like a three-ring circus, with the jug-glers, clowns, and acrobats all doing something quite different from one another. This can be an entertaining performance, but it does absolutely nothing to bring praise to God.

I'm not sure there is a right or wrong way to believe about many of these issues, and I wonder if God is as concerned about all our beliefs as he is about our relationship to him and to each other. The two greatest commandments, "Love the Lord your God with all your heart and with all your soul and with all your mind," and "Love your neighbor as yourself" (Matt. 22:37–39), have to do with relationships, not beliefs.

Our love for one another, resulting in our acceptance of one another, is what will bring praise to God and show the world that we are his disciples (John 13:35) and that genuine love for others is possible.

Most of what I know about acceptance I have learned from my relationship with my friend, Barb. We are as different as two people can be, but a few years ago we finally learned to quit trying to change each other. Now we can learn from each other and celebrate our differences.

We enjoy shopping together in gift shops, record stores, and bookstores. Part of the fun is that we enjoy teasing each other unmercifully about our different tastes. More often than not, a clerk behind the counter is amused.

"You two sure seem to be having a good time," she'll say, with almost a sense of longing in her voice. Everyone wants a close friend, a playmate. I think that my friendship with Barb touches the little girl in other women. We bring a few moments of joy to someone's day, and I truly believe that our acceptance of each other brings praise to God. (I kind of think we keep him amused, too.)

A circus is good for a few laughs, but when it comes down to the basic day in and day out of life, would you rather join the circus, or a loving family where the members enjoy, care deeply for, and look out for one another? The world is watching and listening.

The Alternative

There is only one alternative to acceptance, and that is judgmentalism. If we're not growing in our acceptance of others, we're growing in our judgments of them.

When you first meet an ugly duckling like yourself, you make a decision, whether conscious or unconscious, to judge that person or reach out with acceptance. It can depend on a number of factors: the other's appearance (are his feathers brushed or ruffled?), speech (does she quack or croak?), apparent personality, and response or lack of response to you.

If you never have the opportunity to get to know the person, that first impression will probably be a lasting one. If you do get to know the person, your judgments may be reinforced or your acceptance may grow. It often happens that our judgments fade as acceptance grows (and vice versa).

It is important to understand how we function in our relationships with others so that we can make accepting others the prayer of our hearts and our goal. God can change our judgmental hearts and help us to release our judgments to him. Still, fear holds us back. We are afraid to enter too deeply into another's journey.

Only as I have seen people utterly abandon themselves to the process of letting God love through them, have I seen deep changes take place in individuals, and thus in our world.

Is God big enough to handle the problems that may arise when we choose to involve ourselves deeply in one another's swan processes?

I remember Linda, who became too dependent on me after an evening of bonding. (She had told me more about her past than she had ever told anyone.) There were daily calls, and fabricated crises to pull a response from me. I found myself offering hundreds of excuses and reasons not to be there.

Yes, I cared. I cared deeply. Determined that God wanted to show this ugly duckling her swan reflection, I hung in there. I refused many more pleas for help than I responded to, but we made steady progress. Today, a few years into the journey, Linda has come a long way. She is no longer unhealthily dependent on me, but looks to God for her security.

With time and love, God can effectively work through us. That is, if we can trust him. One strong hindrance to our acceptance of one another is our difficulty in accepting *God,* the one who created us and has called us his "own children." We'll look at that in the next chapter.

"My Own Child"

Jesus Loves the Little Ducklings

> *"He is no turkey," mumbled the mother. "See how beautifully he uses his legs and how straight he holds his neck. He is my own child and, when you look closely at him, he's quite handsome. . . .*

God's pronouncement that you are his "own child" will have real meaning in your life only as you come to the place where you respect God's opinions, where you believe that God's view of you is a positive one. The mother duck said about the ugly duckling, "when you look closely at him, he's quite handsome." This is also God's view of us.

I joined a support group not long ago because I felt I needed outside help with a personal problem. I discovered that many in the group were agnostics, some even atheists. Nice people, but definitely not believers in a personal God. Some of my friends worried that this group's unbelieving philosophies would rub off on me. Quite the opposite happened. Not one who hides my feelings easily, I remember rising to God's defense one night after listening to them blame him for the bad behavior of some human beings.

"Poor God," I moaned, and before I could stop myself, the rest of the words tumbled out. "It's not his fault that we're so weird and mean to each other. God didn't plan for this to happen at all. We're the ones who have screwed it up. I feel sorry for him. He must be terribly disappointed—" I let my words trail off. Everyone stared at me in silence, not knowing what to make of my spontaneous compassion for "poor God."

And then the chorus started.

"Yeah!" one guy said, nodding in agreement. "He's just gotten bad press."

"That's right. He's taken the rap."

"Sad."

Everyone looked thoughtful and meditative as they pondered this new idea, that possibly all the trouble we found ourselves in wasn't God's fault after all.

Has God taken the rap? How much "bad press" have we perpetuated, attributing wars and human atrocities to God's neglect of the planet and all its inhabitants?

God has chosen to let us do what we want to do, to believe what we want to believe about him and his character. Ugly ducklings that we are, we often choose to believe the worst. Otherwise, who would take responsibility for all the terrible things that go on, for all the child abuse, homelessness, and poverty? If God isn't at the bottom of it all, then who is? Could any of this be *our* fault?

When I'm hurting, I search frantically for someone to blame. Do you ever do that? If I stub my toe, I might blame one of my kids in another room for playing his music too loud.

In the world of ugly ducklings, when the big stuff happens—when a loved one dies or a child is sexually molested—God is the logical one to pin it on because, certainly, God is big enough to have kept it from happening. Where was he? Personally, I don't believe God turns his back when we hurt. God gave us free will, the freedom to choose right or wrong, to hurt or to heal, to love or to hate. If we choose to use our free will to kill each other, we can't blame God for that.

For a few years after my divorce, this ugly duckling denied her pain, but it all came to a head when a friend of mine decided to get married.

"What? Is she crazy?" was my reaction. I knew both of these people. I had always considered them sane. "Why would they want to ruin a perfectly good relationship by getting married?"

In spite of my reaction, which was so difficult to conceal, I attended the wedding. I found myself choking on my pain as I struggled to get through the ceremony. But in the car afterward, it all gushed forth. It was God's time to deal with my grief over my divorce.

"My God, he'll hurt her!" I found myself screaming. "What if he turns into a monster?" (Like my husband did. One week after our wedding, he punched me in the mouth over some small thing.) "I can't stand to see that happen to her. No—"

I was sobbing now, remembering my own pain as the larger issue surfaced. "God, how could you create men so strong, knowing they would abuse women? Knowing women couldn't defend themselves?"

It was a milestone in righting some of my wrong beliefs about God: that he didn't care about women, that he made men strong so they could kick us around. As I sobbed out my pain, I felt God's arms around me. I felt my closed heart begin to open, and heard God's reassurance that he created men strong so that they could work hard for the kingdom of God, to fight for truth, to lead, protect, and defend women.

Tough questions abound, like "Why is there evil?" and "Where was God?" Many theologians, writers, and philosophers have expounded on the subject, yet the best anyone has come up with is simply an echo of M. Scott Peck's opening words in *The Road Less Traveled:* "Life is difficult."[1] We might as well just accept that truth, grab life by the gut, and head into the pain.

However, real problems arise when we dump the blame on God, throw up the walls, and form judgments in our hearts.

Over time, those judgments can break down any kind of loving relationship with our Creator. When God says you are his *"own child"* (and handsome at that!), you may not even hear the words.

Let's look for a moment at some things that both hinder and promote our acceptance of God for who he is—Creator of the universe and Lover of our souls.

Who God Is and Isn't

"God is love" (1 John 4:16). If you never learned another thing about God, and this were the only scripture you ever fully comprehended, you would be on the road to understanding who God is.

I knew God was love when my unloving behavior intensified to the place where I knew he had every reason to be really mad at me. Plenty of *people* were. It was like someone had pressed my "nice" button one too many times and sprung all the springs. I can't explain how I knew. But somewhere down deep I felt loved. And the more unglued I came, the more I felt that love. It had to be God.

God is light (1 John 1:5). God became "light" to me when I felt him penetrate the darkness of my despair. It was a gradual awakening, like the dawning of a new day. And in this new day, I knew I wanted to walk in the light of God's presence more than I wanted to hang onto the dark despair.

That's one thing I love about God. He doesn't make us walk out of the darkness all alone; he comes into the darkness to get us and walks out with us.

God is truth (John 14:6). Unlike us, God can't lie. He doesn't even know how, for it goes against the very nature of who God is.

I wanted desperately to believe that "God is truth." But I felt so betrayed by him as I began to see the reality of who I had married and realized that I was about to become a single mom to five kids. I couldn't trust him to lead me truthfully.

And then my understanding of truth began to shift. God is truth whether or not I like what he's doing, even when I'm confused, and whether or not I believe it.

God is justice (Deut. 32:4).

> *Well, here I am. I'm out on the floor again and I can hear the music starting up. Great! I think I'm finally ready to dance. But wait a minute . . . this isn't a floor; it's asphalt! Good grief, we're out on the street!*
>
> *This isn't fair! Somebody turned my nice, safe party out into the streets.*
>
> *This isn't safe; this definitely is not safe. I thought this was going to be an entirely different dance.*[2]

John Fischer's words describe our disillusionment with reality. It's quite the opposite of what we had planned.

So many times I have thought: *This is so unfair. I never planned to be a single parent of five kids. How could God have let such an unfair thing happen? Other people have families—a mom, a dad, kids. I'm alone . . . with five kids. Five kids!*

I expected to get married and stay married. And that's where much of the confusion and pain came in. I *expected*.

But God is just. Fair. So how do we reconcile our preconceived expectations with that? Is God's fairness determined by whether or not God meets our expectations?

God is peace (Eph 2:14). Peace has nothing to do with the state of external circumstances, but is a fruit of the Spirit and an internal state of being. Inner turmoil and chaos were my constant companions until I finally embraced life's confusion and inconsistencies. I had to accept that life, and my life in particular, would never be neat and tidy again. I no longer ran from the confusion—I learned to live with it.

That's when I experienced God's peace. As long as I was running, I never really noticed it was missing. Now I didn't want to be without it for one second.

So God is love, light, truth, justice, and peace. And we have only tapped the surface of God's character. God is much, much, more.

We may pay lip service to knowing all these things about God. But then life deals us a hard blow, and the first words out of our mouths are, "Why, God?" And inside our hearts we cry, "Where were you?" meaning, "It's all your fault. If you cared, it wouldn't have happened."

Is this acceptance of God for who he is?

Now that we have pondered a few things that God is, what is God *not*?

God is *not* an angry giant, eager to squash us earthlings the minute we cross him (Ps. 30:5).

God is *not* a cruel jailer, eager for us to turn our lives over to him so he can throw us behind bars and have total control (Isa. 61:1).

God is *not* burned out on creation, too tired and frustrated to deal with us (Ps. 121:3).

God is *not* too busy running the universe to care about each hair on our head (Luke 12:7).

God is *not* emotionally disengaged from us and our troubles. "As he approached Jerusalem and saw the city, he wept over it and said, 'If you, even you, had only known on this day what would bring you peace . . .' " (Luke 19:41–42).

A huge part of the process of learning to accept God is first the discovery of who he is and then the decision to *believe* what the Bible says about who he is.

God is good. " . . . he cares for you" (1 Peter 5:7).

What God Does (and Doesn't Do)

Who becomes involved in our lives? " . . . it is *God* who works in you . . . ." How? " . . . to *will* and to *act* . . . ." What for? ". . . according to his *good* purpose . . . " (Phil. 2:13).

Recently, a friend and I were discussing what I considered a hopeless situation between two other friends. Then she said, "Well, let's pray for them."

I threw up my hands. "Pray for them? What can God do?

Diane wants it this way and Julie totally disagrees. God can't do anything."

I heard myself. What I really meant was that I didn't think *we* could do anything. As if the outcome of the whole situation depended on two humans. Well, to be sure we were only two sinful humans, but we were also two *praying* humans. And God could do a lot.

God is doing something, whether or not we see or feel it (see Hebrews 11).

The eleventh chapter of Hebrews is filled with the names of biblical characters who were commended for their faith in God's activity in situations when they saw and felt nothing. By faith Noah built an ark. By faith Abraham offered his own son Isaac as a sacrifice. Many of these biblical characters never saw God's fulfillment of his promise to them within their lifetimes. Still, they trusted that God was moving.

God hears us (Ps. 65:2). God's ear is always turned in our direction. Just as we instantly know our children's voices, so God knows our voices. How quickly we are to give up on prayer because things don't turn out the way we planned. We assume that God hasn't heard us. We pray, but don't accept God's answer because it's so different from what we expected. Too often we pray for whatever will make life easier, yet God answers according to what will stimulate the most growth in our love for him and others.

Can we accept the fact that God knows what's best for us?

God teaches us (Ps. 71:17). Unfortunately, God's classroom is not a place where we sit at a comfortable desk and write in brightly colored notebooks. No, God's classroom is a henyard, a bloody battleground where casualties abound and, if we survive, we do so with an abundance of battle scars. Jesus was pierced—for us. Jesus bled—for us. Jesus died—for us. Jesus was resurrected into heaven—a risen Savior, but also a beat-up human being. Do we really think that our life on earth was meant to be a Caribbean vacation?

Once again, these are only a few of the things God does for his children—at least for those of us who let him. God does much, much more.

As Creator

Psalm 148 says,

> *Praise the Lord.*
> *Praise the Lord from the heavens, praise him in the*
> *heights above.*
> *Praise him, all his angels, praise him, all his heavenly hosts.*
> *Praise him, sun and moon, praise him all you shining stars.*
> *Praise him, you highest heavens and you waters above*
> *the skies.*

The psalmist goes on to command praise from the earth, the great sea creatures, the ocean depths, the lightning and hail, snow and clouds, stormy winds, mountains and hills, fruit trees and cedars, wild animals and cattle, small creatures and flying birds, princes and rulers, young men and maidens, old men and children.

"Let them praise the name of the Lord, for he commanded and they were created" (v. 5).

God created all—everything and everyone.

"But this ugly duckling didn't ask to be born," you might think when you are experiencing the pain of life. "It seems like a cruel joke."

I've often wondered about that. What kind of pleasure does God possibly derive from creation now that it's so polluted?

"The Lord . . . will take great delight in you, he will quiet you with his love, he will rejoice over you with singing" (Zeph. 3:17).

Why? Beats me. Maybe it doesn't take too much to make God happy. A heart turned toward him. A mouth praising him. Ears turned to hear God's voice. A newborn baby's smile. A young man and young woman falling in love. An aged couple walking hand in hand along the beach.

Maybe God sees his creation in its original form—very good. Maybe God sees the swans.

> In the beginning God created the heavens and the earth . . . .
> So God created man in his own image . . . .God saw all that he had made, and it was very good . . . .
> And the Lord God commanded the man, "You are free to eat from any tree in the garden; but you must not eat from the tree of the knowledge of good and evil, for when you eat of it you will surely die . . . ."
> When the woman saw that the fruit of the tree was good for food and pleasing to the eye, and also desirable for gaining wisdom, she took some and ate it. She also gave some to her husband, who was with her, and he ate it (Gen. 1:1, 27, 31; 2:16–17; 3:6).

A question: Did God create two sinners? Two ugly ducklings? An answer: God created two swans who *chose* to sin. And it's been our favorite activity ever since.

One reason we have a difficult time accepting God as the perfect Creator is that we choose to deny our responsibility for sin. We hold God responsible for the mess we have made out of his perfect creation. To ask God for forgiveness could be an admission of our own guilt.

As Creator, God deserves our highest praise for his good work in creating potential swans.

As Savior

Although I hate to admit it and wish it were different, my human core is sinful. Max Lucado puts it well in *No Wonder They Call Him the Savior*:

> Evil is paradoxically close to goodness. It is as if only a sheer curtain separates the two. Given the right lure, at the right moment, aimed at the right weakness, there is not a person alive who wouldn't pull back the curtain and live out his vilest fantasy. . . .
> Never did the obscene come so close to the holy as it did on Calvary. Never did the good in the world so tightly intertwine

with the bad as it did on the cross. Never did what is right involve itself so intimately with what is wrong, as it did when Jesus was suspended between heaven and earth.

God on a cross. Humanity at its worst. Divinity at its best. . . .

God is not stumped by an evil world. He doesn't gasp in amazement at the dearth of our faith or the depth of our failures. We can't surprise God with our cruelties. He knows the condition of the world . . . and loves it just the same. For just when we find a place where God would never be (like on a cross) we look again and there he is, in the flesh.[3]

It's mind-boggling that a holy and pure God would let his Son be crucified on a cross for the likes of us ugly ducklings. But he did. And as Jesus walked with sinners long ago, so he does today. It's God's nature. We are his focus, because Jesus is the Savior. I'm learning to make Jesus my daily Savior, watching him "save" me moment by moment from daily felonies and misdemeanors that would otherwise incarcerate me in a prison of my own making. Saving me from the times when:

. . . I lose control and scream at my son for "inconveniencing" me—I watch God save the moment as he whispers, "It wasn't exactly convenient for me to leave heaven and hang on a cross for you, you know." Oh, yeah. I hang my head.

. . . I erect walls between a friend and myself because she hurt me and I want to punish her. God's whisper this time is, "I can understand your pain, but forgive her; she didn't deliberately hurt you. You can work this out." Knowing he's there to help me, I can agree.

. . . God whispers when I'm ready to give up on someone or a situation, or when I'm about to make a stupid decision. Sometimes I listen. Other times I miss the message because I'm noisily quacking and flapping my wings.

Did Jesus walk away from sinners, wringing his hands in despair? No. He offered forgiveness and acceptance. Because that's what a Savior does. Can we accept Jesus in that role? How many times are we going to crash into the milk pail, meeting with utter failure as we attempt to save ourselves? We're already so bruised and bloody. Can it get worse?

As Lord

What does it mean to make Jesus Lord? The New Testament Greek word translated as "Lord" is *kýrios*. Used for God, Jesus, and human beings, it simply means the one who is highest in authority; the one in control.[4] *Authority* and *control* have lots of negative connotations, especially for those of us raised during the sixties. But if we really knew that God loved us and had only our best interests at heart, we could trust that Christ's lordship means freedom.

We're still learning, though, so we go about setting up a self-imposed system of rigid rules and regulations in order to survive life with other ugly ducklings. We trust that our rules will keep us good enough to gain access to God's throne on those occasions when we just can't pull it together and need help, and that ultimately our rules will tip the scales in our favor so we can make it into heaven—even if just barely.

Daniel Taylor summarizes our sad state of affairs:

> He [God] offers us a person and a relationship; we want rules and a format. He offers us security through risk; we want safety through certainty. He offers us unity and community; we want unanimity and institutions. And it does no good to point fingers because none of us desires too much light. All of us want God to behave Himself in our lives, to touch this area but leave that one alone; to empower us here but let us run things ourselves over there.[5]

As Father

Fathers play an extremely important and significant role in our lives as we grow up. I'm not sure we realize just how important a role they may play until we are adults and can't seem to get huge parts of our lives under control, no matter how hard we try. We may even enter therapy, only to discover just how much of the person we are today has been shaped by the way we were treated by our fathers.

The ugly duckling's father is mentioned only once in the story, and that is when the mother duck registers a complaint: "That scoundrel hasn't come to visit me once."

My own father died when I was five years old. And like the mother duck, my mother had nothing good to say about him.

As a grown woman wanting somehow to connect, if only with his memory, I once asked her: "Can you just tell me one good thing about Dad?"

She thought for a moment and then shrugged: "I honestly can't think of anything."

Growing up without a father figure has largely affected the way I relate to men to this day (or *don't* relate to them, as is often the case). We have often heard that the way we relate to our fathers is the way we relate to God. I believe it's true. When I try to connect the image of a father to God, I draw a blank. What's a father?

As an only child, I coasted along in a world of fantasy and make-believe relationships with imaginary characters. These invisible friends were all males and they never left my side. I had total control, of course; sometimes *I* was the one who left.

When I reached my teenage years, though, my imaginary pals didn't cut it. I left them behind and entered into a world of romance and the "real thing." A string of boyfriends kept me quite content until I married one of my infatuations. The "real thing" of a life commitment soon became a nightmare. I bailed out thirteen years later, a shaken, bewildered, and angry child once again. My marriage had turned out to be the biggest disappointment of my life. The ensuing agony, as I dragged my five children and myself through the ashes of what had once been a living, vital organism called a nuclear family, nearly did me in. I'm still recovering.

Why did I get married?

At nineteen years old, I needed a father—desperately. My husband was fifteen years older than I was, and so mature;

surely, he would take good care of me. Besides, he was a Christian—an automatic guarantee. So I put myself totally into his hands. It was a giant mistake. Of course, I wasn't conscious of what I needed back then. This is all in retrospect. How could I have known that God, as my Father, wanted to meet what Dr. Larry Crabb calls my "crucial longings"?

> Think of the basic and most profound longings of the human heart, those desires that must be met if life is to be worth living, and call them crucial longings. We were designed to live in relationship with someone unfailingly strong and lovingly involved who enables us to fulfill the important jobs he assigns. Without relationship or impact, life is profoundly empty. Nothing can fill that hollow core except what we were built to experience. Not imperfect friends, not impressive work, not excitement, not pleasure. Nothing can satisfy our crucial longings except the kind of relationship that only God offers.[6]

What kind of relationship does God offer? "Because you are sons, God sent the Spirit of his Son into our hearts, the Spirit who calls out, 'Abba, Father' " (Gal. 4:6). Even now, I am in the process of making the choice to experience God in the role of Father—my Father. Although the word sounds foreign on my tongue, I am learning to say, "Daddy." And like the mother duck, God thinks I am "quite handsome."

As Friend

Jesus spoke these precious words to his disciples:

> I no longer call you servants, because a servant does not know his master's business. Instead, I have called you friends, for everything that I learned from my Father I have made known to you (John 15:15).

Can you imagine the disciples' joy as they learned that in Jesus' heart was friendship toward them? That their relationship with God was not only vertical, but horizontal? That they not only served and worshiped the exalted Creator, but walked in friendship with the God-man as well?

God actually wants to be friends with ugly ducklings, and created us for that reason. What does it mean to be a friend of God's? What do you share with your best friend? Dreams, passions, hurts, joys, laughter, tears, fun. A walk in the park on a hot summer day, a fire on a cold winter night. Quiet moments of enjoying each other's presence, raucous times of delighting in each other's uniqueness. Do you think that "God said, 'Let us make man in our image, in our likeness,'" so that God could relate, commune, connect—with us?

I'm blessed with many friends, but there's none like God. God has created a lot of folks, but there's none like me. No other relationship in the world is quite like ours.

Friendship with God is the ultimate relationship. The ultimate privilege. The ultimate experience. Nothing will help us cultivate this experience more than acceptance. God has already accepted us—totally. He has called each one of us his "own child." Can we extend the same kind of acceptance to him?

Headed for Trouble

The Practical Side of Change

"Look how ugly one of them is! He's the last straw!" And one of the ducks flew over and bit the ugly duckling on the neck.

"Leave him alone!" shouted the mother. "He hasn't done anyone any harm."

"He's big and he doesn't look like everybody else!" replied the duck who had bitten him. "And that's reason enough to beat him."

"Gloria, I don't quite know how to say this," my friend said quietly, timidly. We were on the phone long distance, and it was hard to hear her. "But what you just said, the way you've been acting lately—well, it feels abusive to me. I feel— assaulted." And she began to cry.

But her quiet sobs barely registered. What did register was that word—*abusive*. Abusive. ABUSIVE! Me? No way.

"That's crazy," I retorted. "You're just too sensitive. You're always—"

Then I "heard" her sobs. I waited. She cried often, after all. I would wait her out. We would talk about her feelings, her hypersensitivity. She would admit that she had exaggerated. She didn't mean *abusive*.

Sure, I was unkind sometimes. I was impatient. I could get frustrated and take it out on others. But—

"It's your tone of voice," she went on. "The way you with-draw. You punish me when I try to express opinions different from yours. You're so strong—I can't fight you. You're controlling—"

She was on a roll now, and even though she was obviously in pain, she was firm, confrontive, and painfully honest.

I couldn't and didn't want to hear. "No. Abusive—that's ridiculous."

But as she continued to pour out her pain, months of sup-pressed feelings about my treatment of her and others, I began to see things from her perspective. Yes, indeed, if I were her, I would feel abused. I knew plenty about abuse. Her accusation was a serious one. I was just coming into touch with what could only be called abuse in my past marriage. I had been reading about abuse because I now realized I was a victim. Could I also be a perpetrator? Yes.

The other ducklings beat him because *"He's big and he doesn't look like everybody else!"* and that was reason enough. I had been beaten in my marriage—spiritually, emotionally, and physically—because in my ugly duckling way, I couldn't please my husband.

Now I was doing to others what I hated the most—judging, punishing, and withdrawing from the ugly ducklings who weren't becoming swans fast enough to please me.

I sobbed and repented for days. I didn't know how to change.

Not knowing how to do something is the best place to be in, for then we have no choice but to rely on God's wisdom. If we think we know how to do it (whatever *it* is), too often we head straight into a big mess. I heard author M. Scott Peck say recently that "Virtually all of the evil in the world has been done by people who *knew* exactly what they were doing."

No, this ugly duckling hadn't a clue as to how to change, how to love others, how to live for God in the world. Up until this point, most of my energy had been spent on surviving the beatings.

Our errors in loving and denial of our abuse usually happen because we think we're above such things. Of course, I *loved* my friend. How could she say I was abusive? What I didn't know was that the abuse I had suffered for so many years now caused me to make self-protection my highest priority. And when a person makes self-protection the goal, loving others is truly impossible. We often take on self-righteous attitudes that sound good and enable us to keep the cloak of self-protection wrapped tightly around us.

We often verbalize two "Christianese" clichés that expose these attitudes.

Cliché number one: "Love the sinner, not the sin." We mean well when we say these words, because we do want to love people. However, the very fact that we speak or even think them reveals that we are making a choice to love—that it's not coming naturally. We are not genuinely identifying with the other person's sinful nature at that point, but are taking on a superior role. To choose to "love the sinner, not the sin" is definitely a step in the right direction. But it's a small one, and not ultimately where we want to be. Our external choices and our internal attitudes can be light-years apart.

Once we fully realize that the sinful nature that causes another person to perform what we think of as an unthinkable action is the same sinful nature that drives us, then "loving the sinner, not the sin" will no longer be the issue. We won't even think those words. We'll just love.

Just because we don't act on a sinful impulse doesn't mean that sin isn't in us. Jesus was "tempted in every way, just as we are—yet was without sin" (Heb. 4:15). If Jesus was tempted in *every* way, do we think we're going to escape certain sinful tendencies inside ourselves? In all honesty, the very reason we have been able to keep up the appearance of being "good" may be our sin. We may care too much what people think of us. Or we may be sinning in secret, where no one sees. We may be in denial, justifying our sins and calling them something else.

The point is that in our ugly duckling selves, we are no better than the out-of-control person who sins blatantly.

Cliché number two: "There but for the grace of God go I." These words, too, reveal where our hearts are. At first glance we appear noble, grateful for God's grace. But at the root of this statement is often an aristocratic fowl, a self-righteous Pharisee. We're saying, "I could be as bad, ugly, and evil as he (or she) is, but I'm not." That's the point—God's grace in the matter is inconsequential.

Would God lavishly favor one ugly duckling with his grace and not another? Is it really God's grace that we're not in a worse situation, or could it be that life simply hasn't beaten us up as much, driving us out of the henyard and into making some bad decisions?

How do we rid ourselves of judgmental, self-righteous attitudes that hinder us from accepting each other unconditionally? What can we do?

Receiving God's Acceptance

We will never be able to cheer anyone else along on their journey to becoming a swan unless we have first come to undersand what God is trying to do in us.

Like the psalmist, we cry out, "what is man that you are mindful of him . . . ?" (Ps. 8:4).

I remember a time in my life when it was inconceivable to me how a holy and awesome God could be "mindful" of me. Not only mindful, but *accepting* of me in my sinful state, to the point of even wanting to be with me. How could that be?

"I'm not cut out to be a Christian," I remember sobbing to a friend. "I'm not made of the right stuff. I know God has had it!"

I felt I had pushed God to the limit. I imagined God saying, "OK, that's it. You've really done it now. You've pushed me to the max." That's where I was.

My friend then whispered the most precious words in my ear: "God isn't even close to being finished with you. He accepts you right where you are."

No matter how hard I tried to change myself, no matter how much I denied my real feelings, no matter how much I hid from myself and others, God knew where I was. I realized that I couldn't be anywhere other than where I was—or now am.

"Then the man and his wife heard the sound of the Lord God . . . and they hid" (Gen. 3:8). Things haven't changed much. We hear God coming and we try to hide. But there is nowhere in the cosmos that God's eyes don't penetrate. All of us get caught with our hands in the cookie jar. Though the evidence is stacked against us, we try to distract God into looking somewhere other than at us and the cookie jar. Or we justify ourselves by claiming starvation and near death—only a cookie will save us. Or we blame God: "God, you made the cookies and put them there; certainly you wouldn't have done that if you didn't expect me to eat them."

"But the Lord God called to the man, 'Where are you?' " (Gen. 3:9). It was a rhetorical question, since God knows everything. Can you and I be honest with ourselves? We will only know God's acceptance when we can admit the truth about where we are. And once we know God's acceptance, we are freed to accept ourselves and others.

Accepting Yourself

Can we accept ourselves? Can we just accept all the bad with the good, pursuing growth and getting better all the time? Of course not. One major reason is that all the other henyard fowl continue to scream at us about how ugly and peculiar we are. They won't put up with us. So we struggle to figure out a way to hide our ugliness and deceive everyone around us.

The raw truth is that the ugly duckling couldn't hide his ugliness. Neither can we. Oh, we may be able to camouflage the junk for a while, but eventually it pops out—usually when we least expect or want it to.

I don't know when I have ever heard a better explanation of a journey into self-acceptance than in Tim Hansel's thought-provoking book, *You Gotta Keep Dancin'*:

> *I've noticed, especially in the past few years, that I tend to avoid books with the word victorious in the title. Somehow they don't seem to speak to where I am. My journey just isn't described in such simple terms. I've struggled with the fact that I am unambiguously Christian and at the same time, unmistakeably human. In fact, my journey has become more human, not less, since I encountered this One called Christ.*
>
> *I think of Howard Butts' profoundly simple question: "Which would you rather have—a Christian reputation or Jesus Christ?" and know again that it is not vital for me to appear to others to be a "victorious Christian." If this process has taught me anything, it is to be who I am in Christ, without images or pretense.*
>
> *Being justified in Christ means, among other things, that I don't have to keep continually justifying myself. I am slowly discovering a radical (in the sense of its etymology, "rooted") kind of self-acceptance—because of God and in spite of my limitations.*
>
> *As I let go of rigid expectations and self-importance, I discovered a new kind of triumph that didn't have to look victorious. One evening I sat down and described it in a poem, "Muffled Triumph."*
>
>> *Mine is only a muffled triumph.*
>> *Joy mingled with still ever-*
>> *Constant pain an unjustifiable*
>> *gladness of merely being alive.*
>
> *The daily confrontations often leave me less than the best.*
>
> *But still something ever new keeps emerging. Hope—now deeper, more enduring. Love—yes, but in unsentimental dailyness. Faith—not enough to move mountains. But just enough to keep me in muffled triumph.[1]*

Hansel calls his ugly duckling self his "humanity." Others call it their "sinful nature" or "original sin." It all means the same thing: our desire to live our own lives apart from God and God's will. Personally, I like the word *depravity*. On the outside, I may look like a pious, upright, aristocratic fowl, but inside I will always struggle with my own depravity. It wasn't until I learned to call my ugly duckling nature by its proper name that God could begin to heal me. We must somehow learn to walk the tightrope of fully recognizing our total depravity, yet at the same time having a deep understanding that we have been made righteous through Christ.

Understanding Your Ugly Duckling Nature

To be *depraved,* according to the dictionary, is to be "corrupt" or "wicked." Our birth into a sinful human nature unfortunately puts *all* of us into the category of the depraved. We have no say in the matter. What we do have a say in is what we are going to do with the awareness of our ugly duckling selves: let that sinful nature control us, or surrender all that we are to God.

If we are not walking in a place of surrender, and especially if we have left the henyard, getting in touch with our depravity can be dangerous. For when we see what sinners we really are, it looks so lonely and hopeless. This is why we work so hard to deny our sinfulness and keep it covered. Deep down, we know that we can't control or change our natures.

I once worked in a place where the team of supervisors refused to admit ever making any errors or mistakes, any mishandling of employees or funds, any type of "ugliness" at all. Yet they demanded total accountability from their employees, and dealt harshly with them as ugly ducklings.

It grieved me deeply. But to be honest, the only reason I even noticed is that it takes one to know one. Ugly ducklings recognize other ugly ducklings, that's all. It would have been so different if they could have understood the good news described in Clinton W. McLemore's book, *Honest Christianity:*

> *Prideful creatures that we are, it is hard for us to acknowledge what we do not like or respect, or what we sense others will*

*disparage. It is so much easier, so much more convenient, at least
in the moment, simply to deny the existence of the distasteful.*

*God, however, is truthful, and to truthfulness he calls us. He
wants us to know ourselves, so that in the process, we can grasp
just how much he loves us. We need not fear what is inside us,
however heinous, however awful, however base. God already knows
all about it, and he loves us anyway—which is, in fact, the good
news of Jesus Christ.[2]*

What does all this have to do with acceptance? It is only as
we accept our depravity that we can make room for that of
others. We will have no tolerance of ugliness in others if we
don't see our own. We may even try to cope by beating them
up the way they have beaten us up.

How do we accept our ugliness, our depravity? We have
such huge problems—wouldn't acknowledging them be to
feel the hopelessness of our lives? The exact opposite is true.
By taking an honest, inside look at our motives and attitudes
on a daily basis, we bring the ugliness out into the light of
God's mercy, where he can help us deal with it.

Thankfully, I now work at a place where employees and em-
ployers alike acknowledge their depravity. How refreshing.
The supervisors hear their employees' grievances, and are willing to make changes, even if it means taking responsibility for
their own ugliness. I watched recently as one of the supervisors apologized for letting another staff member down. And
he followed up his apology with action. This kind of integrity
creates an atmosphere of safety; it's a place where everyone
gets heard, a place where ugliness is accepted and confronted
so all of us can grow, a place of mutual respect between em-
ployers and employees.

It takes a willingness on everyone's part to feel the pain—
the pain inflicted on us by others and the pain we cause others.

Feeling Your Pain

Feeling our pain is what causes us as ugly ducklings to act
on our sinful impulses, to beat up on others. So, is feeling that

pain really a good idea? Wouldn't it be better to suppress and deny our pain so that we can at least live an outwardly "good" life? Sure—if we want to live the life of a Pharisee.

> *Woe to you, teachers of the law and Pharisees, you hypocrites! You clean the outside of the cup and dish, but inside they are full of greed and self-indulgence. Blind Pharisee! First clean the inside of the cup and dish, and then the outside also will be clean (Matt. 23:25–26).*

I understand the pain of a divorced person—I've been there. I have experienced the beating up in a marriage that results in the severing of the relationship.

I am a single parent. I understand being pushed far enough to abuse a child. After a stressful day at work, I come home, exhausted, to five children. Demand after demand meets me. I become more tired and more uptight with each demand. Sometimes I act out sinful impulses. I don't want to, but I do.

I understand the deep kind of depression that leads to suicidal thoughts. I have allowed times of deep pain to weaken my internal resources and my ability to trust God, so that I have almost given up on life itself.

Like everyone else, my journey has had its ups and downs. But the downs were so painful that I couldn't face them. I pretended that life in the henyard was fair and good and easy—and then it all caved in. Life exploded, and I became a near-casualty. Life hurt, and it wasn't until I let myself feel the pecking, beating, and kicking that God could deal with it.

Ironically, the more I have felt the beatings, the stronger I have become, when (and this is an important *when*) instead of employing my own coping strategies, I turn to God in the midst of them. For God does not offer a temporary fix to alleviate the pain, but rather a lasting hope dead in the center of it. This hope makes me able to reach out to you with compassion when you hurt. I can *feel* your hurt and know that it won't kill either one of us, because our hope is based on someone beyond ourselves.

Paving the Road

If I were to choose certain bricks to pave the road of acceptance from me to you, what would they be?

(1) *Love*. I choose to love you, no matter how I feel about your philosophy of life, your spiritual walk, and the way you express yourself.

(2) *Forgiveness*. I choose to forgive you for the offenses done to me in your journey to the swan.

(3) *Faith*. I choose to believe that God is working in your life, in spite of what I may see.

(4) *Longsuffering*. I choose to wait patiently for the completion of God's character (your swan) in you, if it takes a lifetime (and it will).

(5) *Understanding*. I choose to understand your humanness, even though I don't always understand your actions.

(6) *Trust*. I choose to trust you with myself, and if trust is broken, to trust again.

(7) *Openness*. I choose to be open with you, although I have no guarantee that I won't get hurt by doing so.

(8) *Caring*. I choose to care for you (*not* take care of you) as God cares for us—tenderly, watchfully, compassionately.

These bricks represent the ideal, of course. I can commit to these things, but as an imperfect human being, I will fail you miserably at times. I must make choices every day. I want to, I will, and I do.

Part of my responsibility in helping you discover your swan is to keep from forming judgments about you because of the way your ugly duckling nature is expressed. That's so hard to do, and sometimes the judgments pile up before I'm even aware of what I'm doing. How do we deal with one another's ugly areas without piling up resentments and judgments?

Releasing Your Fear

What are we afraid of in our struggle to accept certain people? If we truly desire to resist the urge to beat up on others in their ugliness and to keep from labeling them, and if discovering the swan is our goal, we must identify our fears and face them.

Am I afraid that if I get too close, another's creepy-crawlies will jump onto me, perhaps in the form of a belief, a philosophy, or a way of behaving?

Am I afraid that I will be consumed or swallowed up?

Am I afraid that accepting my teenager in his problem areas means surrendering my parental authority?

Am I afraid that dealing too closely with another's ugliness will surface my own suppressed ugliness?

Am I afraid of losing my image? Will others think I'm like you if they see me loving and accepting you?

Either Jesus didn't have these fears, or he was so sure of his purpose and identity that nothing else mattered. For Jesus was "a friend of tax collectors and 'sinners' " (Matt. 11:10) and was criticized severely for it. He touched lepers and visited them in their homes (Matt. 8:2–3; Mark 14:3). He talked with the woman at the well.

Can we trust that God knows the motives of our hearts as we reach out to accept others? Can we trust God to keep us safe if there is a contagious, wrong belief or an unloving behavior pattern? Can we believe that if our own ugliness surfaces when we accept another, that it is supposed to? And wouldn't you agree that we're in good company if we get criticized for accepting and hanging out with other sinners like ourselves?

If we're going to accept others, we can't walk around paralyzed out of fear that creepy-crawlies might jump from them to us. I will never be able to express the true depth of my gratitude for those who have accepted me even though my personal creepy-crawlies have been in evidence. Because someone (actually, a number of someones) courageously reached out to touch me in the midst of my rottenness, I am more whole.

You may not be afraid of "tax collectors and sinners." How about cancer victims? Drug addicts? Your parents? Where are your limits of acceptance for your gum-chewing, radio-blasting, skateboarding teenager?

Looking Beyond the Sin

What is the need that motivates sin? *Why* did the other fowl in the henyard find the ugly duckling so disgusting in his differentness that they found it necessary to beat him up?

That is where we need to look. For another's bad behavior may trip us up if all we can see is the behavior.

One of my thirteen-year-old son's friends called him the other night, and I listened to Dwight's side of the conversation through the closed door. I never do that. To me, that is akin to reading a child's diary. But the boy who called was one Dwight had gotten into trouble with in the past. Also, I heard Dwight kick the door shut downstairs, cluing me in that this was definitely a very private conversation.

Right or wrong, I held my breath and listened, cursing the washing machine behind me for choosing that moment to shake, rattle, and roll into its spin cycle.

In spite of the bumpety-bump of the washer, I heard these words:

"Yeah. The light will be on. OK — I'll see you at 1:30. Bye."

I stood by the door, my arms crossed in front of my chest, when Dwight emerged, a smug smile on his face. He saw me and froze.

"And just where do you plan to go at 1:30 in the morning?" I asked.

"Uh — just around." Poor Dwight. Caught. Trapped. Defeated — before he even climbed out the window.

I then performed my usual routine — ranting and raving about the weirdos lurking on streets at 1:30 in the morning, bemoaning the betrayal of my trust. I expected him to be safe in his bed at night, and I put him on restriction until his twenty-first birthday.

As the dust settled, we talked about God watching out for him. This was only the second time he had ever planned to sneak out, so he claimed, and the second time he'd been caught—the first time he and his brother had made it to the corner before I called them back.

I wanted Dwight's punishment to fit the crime, so I did indeed restrict him to the house for a sufficient period of time. But that didn't seem to be quite enough in this case. I wasn't sure it would deter him in the future. And how could I continue to show my acceptance of him after this? I was furious.

"Why would he do that?" I asked the Lord the next morning.

"Ask him," is what I felt like God answered.

So I did.

"Dwight, why did you want to sneak out?" I asked later that morning.

"Why?" He looked at me, puzzled.

"Yeah, why? We need to talk a little more about this."

"Well, it's just cool to walk around in the middle of the night. Everyone's in bed, it's all dark and quiet—" He paused, eyed me suspiciously, and then shrugged. "I just felt like it."

I chose to believe him. And if I stepped out of my mother role for a moment, I could identify. I remembered a time in my own teenage years when I had solicited my mother's help to get my window open (someone had painted it shut) because I needed "the fresh air, Mom." My poor mother worked for an hour or two with a hammer and chisel and finally pried it open. I won't go into detail about what I did that night while my mother snored away.

As a night person, I had to admit that I still don't always know when it is time to come home. I understood Dwight. I, too, enjoyed the early morning hours.

"Well, I've decided something," I found myself saying while Dwight waited for me to add even more to the already "unfair and mean" punishment I had dished out. "It's silly for you to go to all that trouble to sneak out just to walk around in our neighborhood. There's nothing to do around here. You should go out with someone who has a car and can take you somewhere where there's something going on."

He continued to eye me warily. "What are you talking about?"

"There's not a whole lot going on at 1:30," I went on. "But we can find something. They have a midnight movie on Capitol Hill, and then we can go to an all-night restaurant . . . ."

Dwight's eyes grew big. "Really?" A smile spread over his face.

"I hope you don't mind going out with your mother. I'll wear my jeans and everything, and try to look cool—and maybe no one will know."

"Are you serious? Wow, that's great."

And that is exactly what we did—after Dwight got off restriction. We had a ball. It definitely brought us closer, and we both came out of it with a deeper understanding of trust in our relationship. The most important thing was that Dwight knew I accepted him right where he was.

Some may disagree with my disciplinary measures. But my desire to accept my son motivated me to move beyond my comfort zone and risk the disapproval of those who might think I was only "rewarding the child's bad behavior."

It's just that something is more important to me than finding the "right" discipline, and that's discovering my role in helping Dwight move from ugly duckling to swan. And focusing on building relationships usually aids this process more than punishing bad behavior does.

Isn't this how God approaches his kids as well? As important as it is to confront and deal with our ugly duckling selves, it is just as important that we recognize the potential swan. We may be sinners, but God sees us as righteous through Christ's blood and relates to us from that place.

6

Bang! Bang!

Dangerous Surroundings

> "Bang! Bang!" Again came the sound of shots, and a flock of wild geese flew up.
>
> The whole swamp was surrounded by hunters; from every direction came the awful noise. Some of the hunters had hidden behind bushes or among the reeds but others, screened from sight by the leaves, sat on the long, low branches of the trees that stretched out over the swamp. The blue smoke from the guns lay like a fog over the water and among the trees. Dogs came splashing through the marsh, and they bent and broke the reeds.
>
> The poor little duckling was terrified.

Seldom do I meet a person I immediately dislike. Joyce was the exception. I was uneasy the minute I first laid eyes on her. I couldn't quite define it, but it's that uncomfortable feeling in your gut. Yet everyone in my circle of friends seemed in awe of her. She knew so much. She was a leader. She seemed so confident. She didn't really acknowledge my existence on the planet until I gained a professional position that she was sure she could make use of. I'm not sure when my discomfort with Joyce turned to real concern over her insatiable hunger for power. It might have been when I heard her make slanderous comments about others one too many times. Or when I watched her rip another person to shreds in my presence. Or when I saw her, one by one, casually dismiss others from her life because they couldn't live up to her high standards of discipline, morality, or professionalism.

Like everyone else, I continued to give her grace, pray for her, and offer "poor Joyce" ongoing forgiveness. "Certainly she doesn't know what she's doing," was the oft-heard comment. "We need to pray for her." And we did. Maybe hundreds of us, since her leadership was so far-reaching.

But then Joyce's hunger for power touched my immediate family, and my concern turned to rage. We had allowed her to get away with abusing us for too long—in the guise of Christian love and acceptance.

Joyce was a Christian, too, and no one had ever confronted her for fear of dividing the body of Christ. Yet for years we had allowed her to attempt to divide *us*.

"It's not fair, God," I sobbed one night as I knelt in front of my fireplace, flinging sticks into the fire as hard as I could, wanting somehow to ease the pain. "She doesn't deserve our forgiveness anymore. She's not worthy—"

I knew where my heart was. I knew I was on the edge of bitterness. I would have to take care of it.

But I knew something else, too. I knew that the day of reckoning had come. We had accepted, offered gushy love, and forgiven long enough. It was time to confront this ugly duckling. *Why me, God?* I asked. *She has hurt lots of people.*

It's then that I knew how God could use the years of abuse I had suffered in my marriage. No one else seemed as sensitized to it as I was—or else they chose not to see because they didn't want to believe it or confront it. Especially not in the body of Christ, where these things aren't supposed to happen, where we're all supposed to be growing in love. But when an abusive ugly duckling refuses to change, and the abuse affects me or those I love, I have to do something.

Dangers abound in situations like this. We can't predict all the dangers ahead of time, but awareness of the kinds of dangers that we may face can go a long way toward helping us courageously choose to confront when necessary.

Like a Fog

It's confusing, isn't it, when the *"blue smoke from the guns"* fogs up our lives and relationships, and we can't see far enough in front of our faces to make wise decisions. We want so much to be loving, caring, accepting people, but when we are, others often seem to take advantage of us.

I cried out to God recently over my kids. "I'm so horribly disappointed. I've always thought that your love could conquer everything and anyone. Something isn't working here. I've tried my best to love, accept, care, and it's all just getting worse. How can I keep going?" It was a foggy day all right.

At that point, my nineteen-year-old son stuck his head in the door and saw my grief. Having some degree of understanding, he walked over and wrapped me up in his muscular arms. "I'm going to make you proud of me some day, Mom. You know one reason I like being around you is you never let me stay where I am. You always challenge me to be more."

Then, as quickly as he had appeared, he was gone. Nineteen-year-old boys can only take so much of a female's emotions, even if that female happens to be their mother.

Yes, he was gone, but I was left feeling a little more hopeful. The phrase he had used stuck with me: "some day." Our reflection awaits all of us. Some day—when the time is right and the fog has lifted—many of us will come face to face with our reflections—and have to decide whether to acknowledge the swan or turn away.

In the meantime, how do we deal with the descending fog? How do we cope with those times of not knowing how far to travel with another ugly duckling or even with ourselves?

The fog can be our friend or our enemy. As our enemy, the danger lies in being so uncomfortable with the blue haze that, instead of waiting for it to lift, we make decisions based on our

panic to get out rather than trusting God *in* the fog and con-
tinuing to move steadily forward.

For example, the fog descended in the situation with Joyce,
and because I didn't know what to do, in some ways I might
have found it easier to continue doing nothing. I remember
praying for guidance every step of the way as I moved through
the fog into the arena of tough love. Every time I took a step,
the fog's density decreased. In retrospect, I now believe that
the fog sometimes descends just because we're in unfamiliar
territory and can't maneuver well.

I remember when my mother was dying of cancer. The fog
was thicker than ever; I didn't know whether to preach salvation to her or simply be an expression of God's great love.
Slowly, gradually, God made it clear. As a zealous new Christian, I had turned her off plenty of times with my obnoxious
preaching. I would ask God to help me express my love—a
new experience for me, since neither my mother nor myself
had ever really done so over the years. As I began to do that,
not only did the fog lift, but I believe that my mother, in her
own way, opened her heart to God before she died.

That's how we make the fog our friend. We embrace the
confusion, knowing that it won't last, but most of all knowing
that times of confusion are major opportunities for growth in
faith and trust in God.

Surrounded by Hunters

No wonder that *"The poor little duckling was terrified."* How
can one little duckling survive in a swamp surrounded by
hunters?

Hunters are everywhere, and sometimes they are in places
where we least expect them. They and their loaded guns spring
up in our churches, our families, and even among our friends.

A hunter's one purpose is to search for game and, having
found it, to shoot. How can we survive when hunters are all
around us?

We survive by hiding, of course. I'm certainly not going to poke *my* head out of the reeds if it's me they're after. Although they usually champion a particular cause, sometimes hunters simply get trigger-happy. They shoot at anything.

I remember attending one particular religious convention in a big city. During an off moment, a friend and I escaped to the Hard Rock Cafe down the street. Just as I bit into my juicy hamburger, a brood of convention conferees swept by our table. One of them recognized us, and she backtracked with a huge "religious" smile on her face.

"Oh, God must have told you the same thing he told us," she gushed. "We're here praying for these people, too." She eyed our quiet corner table, and then our hamburgers, with suspicion. Her smile faded just a bit. "Isn't it wonderful to be able to be an influence for God in a place like this?"

Did she suspect that we were eating our hamburgers, not praying? I also couldn't help wondering if *she* were there to eat a hamburger, too, and just telling us she was praying because she thought that's what was expected of her. I found myself feeling a little sorry for her.

Can't we ever just be human? You know, eat a hamburger, sail a boat, and listen to music without getting religious? On the heels of feeling sorry for this woman, I also realized that I felt a little hunted—spied upon, watched.

The cause here was "witnessing." We were in that city to "witness," not to eat hamburgers. My friend and I were suspect because we weren't overtly witnessing, and I felt like a hunter was stalking us.

Oh, I've done my share of hunting, too. But the truth is, I didn't like being the big, scary person who caused ugly ducklings to run for cover whenever I showed up. Sadly, some people actually enjoy exercising this kind of power over others.

I believe that as we become aware of the hunter inside of us (with gun always loaded, beady eyes constantly scanning the bushes for prey), God desires that we oust that hunter as quickly as we can before he does any damage.

The real danger with hunters is that they tend to multiply; they want to pull us into the chase. We must resist this pull, choosing instead to walk in integrity, to champion one cause—the journey of the swan. We must refuse to carry a gun to be used on anyone we don't understand.

God's love is the only weapon we need.

The Awful Noise

Henry David Thoreau once said, "You cannot hear music and noise at the same time." I have listened to the body of Christ make noise for a long time. And I have made lots of noise myself. We have kept up such a steady stream of noise over such a long period of time that I'm not sure anyone even hears us anymore. We have become a dull roar in the background of our busy lives.

I don't know about you, but I'm ready for the music. The *"awful noise"* drowns out the pure music that God means for us to hear; his whispers, his heartbeat, his rhythms.

If we can't hear music and noise at the same time, then we're going to have to order our lives so that the noise becomes more distant and music moves into the foreground.

I see three major kinds of noise that interfere with God's music.

(1) The first kind of noise is *voices from outside*.

Certain folks, including my children, tend to see life pretty much in black-and-white terms, and they want me to see it that way, too. They have already decided which ugly ducklings are worth saving and which ones should be thrown out; which events the ugly duckling should process along the way, and which events he should suppress or ignore; and who the ugly duckling can take with him on his journey and who he can't.

The more we listen to the voices from outside, the more they invade our lives and the louder they become. Victims have a certain look that seems to invite the outside voices to enter, sit down, and direct their lives. The only way to stop this invasion is to stand up and say, "That's enough! From now on I will listen only for the music, and if you don't have a pure note to bring me, then you're not welcome."

I have a friend who did this. For many years she allowed her husband, her kids, her friends, and her coworkers to tell her what to do with her life. She needed so desperately to please everyone that it became an addiction to approval. She finally realized that letting them impose their life agendas on her wasn't doing her any good at all. But when she screamed, "Stop!" no one knew quite what to do. Scrambling to make sense of it, they accused her of rebellion, wondered if she was losing her sanity, and demanded that she "shape up" and listen. After all, she always had before. It was an awful noise, but so far, that ugly duckling is holding her own.

(2) The second kind of noise involves what I call *managing our junk*.

Our material possessions are an external distraction to our journeys because they keep us so preoccupied. We are constantly buying, cleaning, repairing, trying to find a place to store, and worrying about losing, our junk. I hate this about myself. Recently I bought my "mid-life crisis" car, a spotless, white sports car. I find myself going to the window frequently, looking out to make sure it's still there. But when I went out of town for a few days and asked a friend to check up on it while I was gone, to make sure no one was scratching it or anything, I knew the car had become a problem. I don't even worry that much about my *kids* when I leave town! It's truly disgusting.

Junk creates its own external noise and clogs our head with thoughts that distract us from what is really important.

(3) The third kind of noise is *inside us*. Our internal dialogue with ourselves creates unbelievable noise in our heads that we can't seem to turn off, no matter how much we try. The internal dialogue includes statements like: "Give up. You're not making any progress anyway." "What you did was pretty dumb. Actually, *you're* pretty dumb." "Look at that ugly

duckling over there. You're a hunter, so you better get your gun."

And the awful noise goes on, and on, and on.

I am much more aware of the noise than I used to be. So now I'm better equipped to turn it off and hear the music. The more I hear the music, the more I *want* to hear it, and the more the noise bugs me. We grow.

Excuses Abound

Once we're on this journey, we are so eager to "do it right," to give unconditional acceptance to one another, that we can too easily begin to make excuses for the ugliness that doesn't change and that doesn't look like it's going to change in the near future.

My friend Marie is from Germany, and she pretty much gets to treat her friends any way she wants, because "that's how they do it in Germany." We're always making excuses for her.

I'm not sure when I first noticed it; all I know is that after another sharp retort from her one day, I walked away, but later exploded to another friend.

"I'm tired of Marie's bluntness," I said. "You know what she said to me today?" But before I could finish my story, my friend defended her. "That's because in Germany, they—"

I wouldn't listen to that anymore. "That's not fair. She gets to sin against people whenever it's convenient because in Germany they do whatever. But I don't have any excuses. I don't get to treat people that way. And if I do, I have to repent." I continued to grumble, knowing that this was my problem and that I needed to do something about it.

Part of doing something about it is to remember not to take Marie's words personally; she talks to everyone that way. Still, I can't let her get away with that. Sometimes I have to say, "Ouch!" so she will know how she affects people. That's what I've been doing. The other day she called and, out of the blue, said, "Something's wrong. I find myself yelling too much in class (she teaches gymnastics to girls). They're starting to say things, and a couple of them have even dropped out. I'm scaring my own kids, too. I'm not sure what it is, but I'm praying God will show me." Enough of us had said "Ouch!" that she had to stop and look at herself.

We do ourselves and others no favors when we continue to make excuses for unloving behavior.

Do you find yourself excusing ugliness a lot?

"Don't cry, honey. That's just your father's gruff way. He really has a heart of gold."

"Oh, that's just Gretchen. She's always been like that. She'll never change."

"Your mother just has one of her headaches again. Don't take it too seriously."

"He acts that way because he was raised without a dad."

"It's because she was abused—"

All of these excuses are OK for a while. Everyone gets to blame others, headaches, or abuse, and be ugly—for a while. We all have reasons why we act in unloving ways, and it helps to understand these reasons. However, if we're not careful, our reasons become excuses (especially if they work), and our growth is hindered.

I remember the day I woke up and realized that my ex-husband and my mother were not to blame for all my problems. They may have started the ball rolling, but it was my ball now, and I needed to roll it toward wholeness.

Boundaries

One weakness in us that keeps us from rolling the ball toward wholeness is our inability to set boundaries. The desperate need for acceptance in our ugliness keeps us from drawing the line at another's unloving behavior toward us.

The ugly duckling kept setting himself up. He constantly put himself in situations with the kinds of folks that would hurt him. This wasn't because he was stupid, but because he was desperate for love and acceptance. In a sense, for survival's sake, the ugly duckling did set boundaries; he left whenever it became apparent that someone intended to abuse or violate him.

Before he sees his reflection and is strengthened, the ugly duckling is by nature in a vulnerable position. He is easily hurt. But because of his needs, he can't seem to set the necessary boundaries before abuse causes much damage.

As children, we are in need of love and acceptance from our parents, and we can't set boundaries. If our parents don't, won't, or can't, then we're helpless. As far as I know, my own mother never had established boundaries, although other than one time of reading my diary without my permission, I don't particularly remember that she violated me.

As a result, I felt it keenly when my husband, who also had no boundaries, regularly violated mine. He wanted what he wanted when he wanted it.

I remember walking into the garage one day where he was cleaning. He had just handed a stuffed frog of mine to a little girl on the sidewalk. I assumed that he was showing it to her.

I turned away for a few minutes, and when I turned around again, the little girl was gone. I looked around and noticed that my frog was, too.

My ex-husband was whistling a cheery little tune.

"Where's my frog?" I asked.

"Huh?" He looked puzzled for a moment. "Oh, you mean that old stuffed animal I just gave to that little girl?"

"You *gave?*" I said. I started to choke up.

"Yeah. What's the matter?"

"My grandmother gave me that frog." My grandmother had recently passed away.

It was like he hadn't even heard me. He shrugged. "It's more blessed to give than to receive. You can get another one, if it's that important to you."

"No, you don't understand. My grandmother—"

"Your grandmother's dead. Look, the little girl was delighted. Don't be so selfish."

Selfish. Was I being selfish? It was only the first of many similar situations. He would violate my boundary, and when I cried "Ouch!" I was accused of being selfish. "Un-Christlike." "Frigid." "Unspiritual."

But I needed him to approve of me, of course. I needed him to think that I was beyond caring that I had lost a silly little stuffed frog, especially since it had made a child so happy. What was wrong with me? I could remember the Christmas my grandma had given it to me. But my frog was gone.

I started suppressing a lot of pain, every time a boundary was violated. I needed his acceptance too much.

It works the other way, too. When I want to give acceptance, sometimes I ask too many questions and prod too deeply. I'm learning to be more careful, more sensitive.

I remember one time when my teenage son was learning to set boundaries. I asked him a question.

He started to answer, as he always did, when suddenly he stopped. "Wait a second. Why should I tell you that?"

I shrugged, realizing something myself. "You don't have to answer all of my questions," I told him.

He looked relieved. "You're right." I had just given him permission to have his boundary.

7

"You Don't Understand Me"

Accepting the Differences

"You don't understand me!" wailed the duckling.

*"And if I don't understand you, who will? I hope you don't
think that you are wiser than the cat or the old woman—not to
mention myself. Don't give yourself airs! Thank your Creator for
all He has done for you. Aren't you sitting in a warm room
among intelligent people whom you could learn something from?
While you, yourself, do nothing but say a lot of nonsense and
aren't the least bit amusing! Believe me, that's the truth, and I
am only telling it to you for your own good. That's how you
recognize a true friend; it's someone who is willing to tell you the
truth, no matter how unpleasant it is. Now get to work: lay some
eggs, or learn to purr and arch your back."*

"I think I'll go out into the wide world," replied the duckling.

"I broke his shoulder," Ruth said.

I choked on my minestrone soup. "You *what?*"

"I grabbed a two-by-four on my deck and hit him. I broke
his shoulder. He had to go to the hospital."

I studied my friend to see if she was kidding. There is always
the possibility of gross exaggeration when one is talking about
what one would like to do to one's ex-husband. She wasn't.

"You really broke his shoulder?" I pictured the petite

woman across from me swinging a block of wood into the burly man who was her husband. "You must have been really mad."

"I've been that mad."

"Really?"

The tragic story that unfolded had actually begun years before. A married couple torn by strife, eventually divorced, and now separately focused on one thing and one thing only—their blue-eyed, four-year-old son who was constantly shifted back and forth between them. They could never agree on anything concerning him, and their last disagreement had turned violent. Knowing some of Ruth's history in her marriage to an abusive husband, and having been married to an abusive man myself, I could understand strong reactions. I had never broken any part of my husband's anatomy, but then again maybe I just never had the opportunity presented to me. Anyway, the point is that I need to stay true to my commitment to walk alongside Ruth in her journey to becoming a swan.

How can I best do that? How do I stay committed to my friends when they may be going crazy, if only temporarily? How do I stay committed when a friend's behavior is affecting me in abusive ways? And how can I empathize with another's behavior when that behavior is far removed from anything I myself have ever experienced?

Response

When someone makes an announcement like my friend Ruth did, how *should* I respond? Should I reach across the table, pat my friend's hand, and say kindly, "Dear, did you know you committed a violent act and need to repent now?"

Should I gasp and scream, "I thought you were a Christian!" Should I keep my mouth shut and hope that my silence will speak my disapproval—that is, if I disapprove. Or is approval or disapproval the issue? My friend was just giving me highlights of the previous evening. Rather intense ones, it's true, but she wasn't asking for advice.

Actually, I gave up the "shoulds" a long time ago. These days I don't worry too much about how I *should* respond. I just try to listen and care the best I can.

The hen couldn't have responded more poorly to the ugly duckling's wail of *"You don't understand me!"* She told him quite plainly: "You're dumb." "Don't throw a tantrum." "You should be thankful." "You're a grumbler." "Do something positive with your life—be like me."

All this because the ugly duckling verbally expressed his longing to do what ducks do—swim. On its own, the hen's response was cruel and self-righteous. But it was especially devastating because of what the duckling was being criticized for—just being himself.

When I became a Christian, I loved the new sense of belonging to this large and wonderful family of God. Raised as an only child, I was more than familiar with isolation. Now, to be part of a warm, caring community—it was more than I had ever hoped for.

The ugly duckling, too, hoped he had found a warm, caring community when he found the old woman's hut. I'm not sure why he stuck around when she announced her plans for him: *"Now we shall have duck eggs, unless it's a drake. We'll give it a try."* Maybe he thought he could lay eggs. Maybe he even tried.

I tried, too. I tried too hard and for much too long. The shock came not so much when I discovered that I really was just an ugly duckling and couldn't lay eggs, but when I was forced to leave the comfort of community because the pressure to conform to an image impossible for me was too great. I, too, had to go out into the wide world.

The issue might be sin. Or it might be simple ignorance of something we don't understand. It might be a decision or a value system that we believe goes against biblical principles.

When someone behaves in a way that demands or requires us to respond, do we do so in a way that we proudly perceive as upholding righteousness? Do we quote scripture, voice our disapproval, and stand up for godly principles? We may even perceive ourselves to be modern-day prophets and boast to our friends that "we spoke the truth in love."

But once the confronted person is gone, the question that should haunt us is: Which is more important—relationships or principles? Who is more important, people or a standard? Maybe it's both. Maybe choice is unnecessary.

Jesus' response to *sin* was to die on the cross for *people*. Because of this, I conclude that Jesus values people above all else. What do *I* value most? Why are so many Christians today obsessed with keeping the law and making sure everyone else stays in line, too? Jesus died to set us free from the law. Isn't it tragic that when we become Christians, we focus on keeping the dead law instead of accepting our freedom?

For those of us who tend to respond like the hen, it is that very response that reveals our tenacious fear of breaking the law rather than valuing people.

Looking Beyond the Behavior

Behavior that confuses us, whether it's ours or someone else's, is scary. The key is to resist focusing on the behavior. Instead, focus on (1) how God might like to help us grow, and (2) how we can best love the other person.

In relationships, everyone's issues come into play. I love watching how God dovetails our journeys when we are aware of his involvement. That is, if we are focused on what he is doing and not on the behavior. When we focus on the behavior, we miss the miracles.

We miss miracles all the time, and not only because we're focused on behavior. It also depends on whether we want to grow or not and how badly we want to grow. I have a couple of dear friends who have consistently looked beyond abusive and self-destructive behavior in this ugly duckling, committing themselves instead to bringing to the surface the insecurity, rage, and low sense of self-worth behind the behavior. My friends know that behavior is always a result of a deeper belief or feeling. At the right time, we address the behavior in one another because it illuminates these deeper issues.

Because of the abuse in my marriage, I still experience occasional panic attacks. Something that just about always brings on a panic attack is an invitation to a wedding or wedding shower or anything remotely connected with the big "M." Oh, every once in a while I feel fine about it all, and I breeze through a marriage event. But most of the time I don't show up at certain social gatherings, and my close friends know why.

Last summer my best friend, who thought (and hoped) I was further along than I was, lost sanity for a moment and sent me an invitation to her daughter's wedding reception.

Not to the wedding, just to the reception. I stared at the invitation in my hand after pulling it from the mailbox.

"Just the reception," I assured myself. "No big deal." But somewhere inside I knew it was a bigger deal than I was letting on. I tucked the invitation away in my filing cabinet, thinking I would deal with it later.

My friend, of course, was totally caught up in the wedding preparations, and I cheered her on, genuinely happy for the bride (and so happy it wasn't me).

The day before the wedding found me at the mall buying a gift, wrapping it, and contemplating what I would wear the next day. A friend called to see if I wanted to ride to the reception with her and her husband.

"Oh no," I quickly refused. I knew I wanted my own car there. Something wasn't right.

The next day I drove to the reception, stuck my head in the door of the restaurant where all the celebrants were gathered, and started hyperventilating.

"This is absolutely ridiculous," I told myself. "It's only a wedding reception, for pete's sake. It's not contagious or anything." But my rational mind had no effect at all on the neurotic palpitations of my heart. I dashed to the guest book, scrawled my name (at least I could say I had been there), parked my gift, and scurried back to the safety of my car, where I burst into a torrent of tears.

"Will I ever be well?" I screamed.

When my friend and I discussed it later that week, she expressed her own disappointment at my inability to truly share in and celebrate her joy. But most importantly—

"It's OK," she told me. "You did the best you could."

To anyone who had viewed only the external behavior, I would have looked rude, as if I didn't think it worth my time to attend my best friend's daughter's wedding. But my friend understood. Even though she was disappointed, she was able to look past the external behavior and see the ugly duckling struggling to let a swan emerge.

Accepting the "Wild" Times

A group of my friends and I had gathered at a home one night to play some games. It was a fun night. These were all deeply spiritual women, leaders in their churches.

One game got a little out of hand, and the most "spiritual" one of the group (at least in our eyes) suddenly screeched in fun, "Put the card down, you _____ !"

Everyone gasped. Then we realized that she was quoting a line from a movie we had recently viewed, and we breathed a little easier. Then someone else repeated the phrase.

The phrase was tossed around for the rest of the evening by a few of the women, all in fun. I watched with interest, knowing that both guilt feelings (among the participants) and judgment (among the nonparticipants) would follow.

I was right. When we got together the next week, everyone was ready to analyze the evening.

"That was just terrible, that we could so easily fall into such a subtle trap of Satan's."

"And continue all night long."

"And enjoy it."

Clucking of tongues. Shame. Heaps and piles of guilt.

To me, it was simple. A bunch of religiously minded women who had never dared speak a particular bad word, experienced one terrifying, compelling, delightful moment of letting go. Spontaneity. Freedom. Never mind the word—it was irrelevant. But shamed to the core, I knew they would never give up control like that again.

To my knowledge, they never have.

It might be a wild shopping spree where you spend too much money. You might feel a strong urge to dance the night away. Or to read a racy novel. Or to skip church one Sunday morning for absolutely no reason.

Sound dangerous? I call them wild times. Some call them rebellion. Others wring their hands and call a twenty-four hour prayer vigil.

Wild times come and go. But we all think we know what's best for *others* in their wild times.

The ugly duckling simply expressed his love of the water, and the hen quickly retorted, *"You must have gone mad."*

The duckling expressed his authentic self and was immediately deemed crazy. To me, this sounds all too familiar. The more we move away from the accepted mold and become the unique swan that God intends us to be, the more others may think us insane. The truth is, the more I pursue the journey of the swan and come to know myself, the more sane I feel. Yet when others express disapproval or displeasure with my particular swan process, I sometimes falter.

"Who really are the sane ones?" I might cry out. It scares me to think it might not be me. Yet I'm confident that this ugly duckling was destined to be a swan. The journey is a struggle. It is definitely not a smooth, unruffled, clean process. It's bumpy. It's messy. It ruffles feathers—mine and everyone else's. I happen to believe that every ugly duckling who is committed to the moment of seeing his reflection will experience wild times. If we are having trouble accepting another's wild times, it may mean we're ready to have one of our own.

Most of us don't allow ourselves to claim wild times. Times like this make us feel out of control. The paradox is that only as we give up control can we ever regain control and, ultimately, regain our freedom. Wild times aren't excuses to hurt ourselves or others. They're opportunities to exercise our freedom in Christ. " 'Everything is permissible,'—but not everything is beneficial. 'Everything is permissible'—but not everything is constructive" (1 Cor. 10:23).

Wild times don't have to be destructive. We don't have to fear them. God dwells in the wild times as he does in normalcy. Welcome these times for yourself and others. They are a necessary part of the swan's journey.

Understanding

In troubling times, when I know I am being misunderstood by significant others in my life, it comforts me to think about Jesus. Jesus had to be the most misunderstood person who ever lived. He tried to teach his disciples profound truths about life and God and his purpose on earth, but they were just too earthbound to get it—too small-minded, too narrowly focused.

Of all the things the duckling could have cried out when criticized for being himself, his wail was *"You don't understand me!"* In our own search for someone to understand, at times we become desperate. Why is being understood so vitally important to us?

To me, having another's understanding means I'm not alone, someone cares about who I am, and someone knows and accepts me as I am right now.

Understanding or the lack of it touches us at our core. Are you ever appalled at your own behavior, with you yourself not understanding why you do certain things? It's rather wonder-ful when someone comes along and puts it all together for you, helping you understand yourself.

In my search for sanity, my relentless and probing questions have led me to an understanding of myself.

One big issue in my life has been my fear of abandonment. Everyone has this fear to a degree, but when I have felt it kick in, some of my behavior has at times been what could only be called bizarre. I get overly possessive in my relationships. I become controlling one minute and withdrawn the next. I need more attention than ever.

As I looked deeper, I could see that my childish behavior was driven by some childhood issues that I had never resolved. My mother had three children. She gave my older brother away to her parents, who raised him, and put my younger brother up for adoption—twice. She retrieved him once, only to give him away again a year later.

Understanding the deep fear of abandonment I suffered as a child helped me empathize with myself, giving myself the time I needed to work through this fear.

Knowing that God will never abandon me is one truth I tell myself when panic hits. If a person chooses to leave me, it has nothing to do with my worth. I go through a series of truths in my mind. Most of all, I can give myself a break now because I know where the rest of the fear originated.

So what does understanding ultimately accomplish?

It defuses fear, the kind of fear that makes us self-destructive or murderous toward others. Without understanding, we lack empathy, and without empathy, anything can happen.

But how do we achieve understanding of someone's behav-ioral issues when we just don't understand?

We may ask question after question, questions that come not from a codependent need to change the other person, but from a desire to call forth the swan inside.

Phrase these questions carefully, delicately.

I sat down with a friend one day. She was having an affair with a married man. This is something that I have a hard time understanding. I know how affairs can happen, but I can't understand why married people betray their spouses. What made my friend's affair even more difficult for me to understand was her answer to my first question.

"Do you love him?"

"Oh, no," she answered. "It just kind of happened."

I knew then that her journey to her swan had been detoured—or maybe even temporarily derailed.

"Don't you ever feel used?" I wondered. "I think I would. Or like you're using each other?"

I wanted to understand what would make her sell her soul this way. More importantly, I wanted her to have to think consciously about what she was doing and why.

We may search for a place of identification. What have we experienced in life that places us alongside other ugly ducklings? That is what unites us with the rest of humanity.

When someone confided in me once that she was a cocaine addict, I immediately searched for a place of identification. But it was difficult for me to imagine getting hooked on cocaine. I would be too scared to take the first snort, or whatever they call it.

I knew she was having a hard time in her life, even though she was a Christian and loved God with all her heart. Then I remembered the first years after my divorce. I drank alcohol almost every evening—just to dull the pain and cope with single parenting. I understood my friend only too well.

We may let ourselves feel *with* others. Our empathy will often unlock our mental incapacity to understand something at a rational level.

We quit worrying about the "right" response and let ourselves experience the real and true one—the one that comes from inside. If we don't understand, we can say that: "I don't understand, but I want to. Can you help me?"

If we feel judgment, we can acknowledge that to ourselves. We might even want to go as far as to say: "I've always judged people who did that. I don't want to do that anymore. Help me understand your thinking on this."

There are times when, no matter how hard we try, we just can't understand. At those times, love is still what matters the most.

"I don't understand, but I love you. And I'm committed to your journey."

But how wonderful, how safe, how comforting when the light dawns in another's eyes and we hear, "I understand."

Surrendering Responsibility

The second greatest commandment is to love one another. How free we would feel if that were *all* we concentrated on doing in relation to each person in our lives! We are only responsible to help others discover their reflections, not to launch them.

What happens when you sit down with another person and unexpectedly that person pours out a horror story that brings out the fight in you? Your feelings intensify the more the other person talks. You know some kind of response is necessary. You may be the kind of person who (1) *can't handle conflict,* so you say nothing. But you walk away, feeling guilty, like you failed both God and the other person.

Or you might be the opposite, the kind of person who (2) *says everything and more.* Your nervousness causes you to talk incessantly, dispensing all kinds of advice and boring data about the issue up for discussion.

You may be somewhere in the middle, the kind of person who (3) neither says too much nor too little, but *seizes this opportunity from God to "share" all the scripture you've learned* and make sure the other person hears. You feel responsible to wave the red flags, sound the alarms, and call in the troops.

In the end, the old woman, the hen, and the cat were too

much for the ugly duckling. He felt overwhelmed. The hen-yard was just too much.

The journey toward becoming a swan is a precarious one. No one can navigate it for another. Each ugly duckling is responsible only for him or herself. The rest of us are only responsible to glide by on occasion, touching the ugly duckling's longings.

We are more fragile than we realize in our journeys. Those of us who look the toughest are often the most fragile. We can so easily affect the delicate balance of God's work in an ugly duckling's life by aggressively taking on the responsibility for the other's journey and ultimately chasing him away. I've seen this happen over and over again. The ones who are left try to make sense of the duckling's departure. They say things like: "He sure had a bad attitude." "She was never serious about changing." "God is separating the sheep from the goats, weeding them out." "He didn't want to hear the truth." "Guess she didn't really want to live for God, after all."

Sometimes the above conclusions about a person are true. But more often, I believe, a "hen" has taken too much responsibility and wounded a duckling. In order to survive, the duckling has no recourse but to leave the scene and continue her journey.

True Wisdom

Thousands of years ago, God gave King Solomon the opportunity to ask for everything he wanted. The king asked for "a discerning heart," better known as wisdom, to govern God's people (1 Kings 3:9).

We may not be "governing" God's people, but we are definitely striving to love and live with them so as to help them fulfill God's purpose for their lives. To assist another in discovering the swan inside is the most powerful way to express God's love. For this awesome task we need wisdom.

Every once in a while, a fragile person or situation comes

along where I know that moment-by-moment wisdom is a must. I'm in one of those situations right now. This person's behavior is making me crazy because she is so close that everything she does affects me. I could freak out over it all; instead I pray for wisdom. I am learning a lot about wisdom—how it feels and what it looks like in different situations. This is what I'm discovering:

(1) *Wisdom waits and watches* before taking action. Timing is everything. When everything, or even one thing, is flying out of control in someone's life and we want to hang in there, it's so important that we watch and listen for signs to know what to do and when. Yesterday, knowing we couldn't talk at the moment, I wrote a letter to the person mentioned above.

(2) *Wisdom is supernatural,* so my first reaction to a person's behavioral issues is probably not the most godly one. Although Jesus definitely experienced reactions, like overthrowing the money-changers' tables in the temple, he wasn't a reactionary. Jesus always waited for his Father, and did only what he saw the Father doing. Peter, on the other hand, is a great example of a reactionary. He pretty much reacted to circumstances.

(3) *Wisdom desires God's highest purpose* in a relationship or situation and will always hold out for that, no matter what is happening externally. Wisdom looks beyond the surface, keeping God's purpose in mind, and responds (not reacts) accordingly.

We can count on God's wisdom to pull us through the most difficult situation regarding another's behavior and how it affects us. If we can rely on God's wisdom instead of our limited human knowledge and strength, we can relax and trust the other person to God, since God knows best how he wants it all to turn out for everyone.

I find it rather wonderful that God wants to involve us in the swan-making journey. But that is the very thing that sobers me—God trusting me with his precious ugly ducklings.

I *do* have an influence on their journey to discovering the secret of the swan.

So I plod on, listening to another's heartache, comforting in crises, concentrating on my part in the swan journey in their lives. And I pray for wisdom, knowing that is our only hope.

8

The Duckling Was Afraid

Learning from Negative Experiences

> *The children wanted to play with him. But the duckling was afraid that they were going to hurt him, so he flapped his wings and flew right into the milk pail. From there he flew into a big bowl of butter and then into a barrel of flour. What a sight he was!*
>
> *The farmer's wife yelled and chased him with a poker. The children laughed and almost fell on top of each other, trying to catch him; and how they screamed! Luckily for the duckling, the door was open. He got out of the house and found a hiding place beneath some bushes, in the newly fallen snow; and there he lay so still, as though there were hardly any life left in him.*

After everything he had faced on his journey, the duckling had every reason to be afraid. He had suffered through the taunts in the henyard, the hunters' guns exploding around him, the vicious dog's jowls—and finally, when he thought he had found a safe place, shame was heaped upon him by the cat and the hen.

When I began my divorce proceedings, the women's ministry board at my church closed down the Bible study I was teaching.

"We can't continue to support this Bible study," my pastor's wife explained. "You have taught these women to challenge and question everything—now we've got a bunch of rebellious women on our hands, and I'm not sure what to do. We never realized this was going on—how your rebelliousness was influencing them."

My *rebelliousness?* What made questioning rebellious? I loved the women in my Bible study, and they loved me. We enjoyed exploring God's Word together, questioning and evaluating our current belief systems, pondering old truths and wondering how we could make them relevant to our lives today. That was rebellious? I had always thought that rebellion was an attitude of the heart that refused to listen to God. We had never done that, and I was confused.

When I needed it most, my support network began slipping away. And while all of this was happening, my husband graciously promised to pray for my "rebellious heart" so that I would come back and "submit" to his leadership.

But I had never thought of my leaving him as being an act of rebellion; I was just so worn down from his emotional, physical, and spiritual woundings. I was doing the only thing I knew I could do to survive. Was that rebellious?

By this time I had heard the word *rebellious* too many times. If everyone–all of these spiritual giants I knew—thought I was rebellious, then maybe I was. If breaking away from abuse was rebellious, then the shoe fit. If exploring, questioning, and challenging beliefs on the basis of God's Word was rebellious, then I guess I was guilty.

But then the line of questioning continued for me. Wasn't rebelliousness being anti-God? Was I anti-God as a result? Like the ugly duckling, I was now alone—and terrified.

Fear of Harm

The farmer's children only wanted to play with the ugly duckling, but in their hasty approach, with leaps and bounds, screeches and flailing arms, they frightened the duckling.

I can understand. In my times of panic, I have crashed into

hundreds of milk pails, butter bowls, and flour barrels. Some of my pursuers had definite plans to harm me, but many only wanted to play. It didn't matter—I didn't stop long enough to try to discern the difference; I ran from them all.

When we're afraid, we don't have many choices about how we view things. We view everything through our fear. And we just can't trust anyone.

Is it fear of harm, fear of being wrong, or fear of failure? Whatever the fear, I have watched it paralyze individuals and entire groups of people until they couldn't make a move without looking over their shoulders to see who was watching.

I know fear. It drove me. Everywhere I turned I saw monsters waiting in the shadows, leaping out at me to tell me what to do, how to think, how to feel, where to go, how to live, who to talk to, what to listen to, and, eventually, how to die.

Some of these monsters were real people, others were voices in my head. Either way, it was my reality at the moment, and I lived in terror of the past, the future, and especially the present.

The Mess

The duckling didn't deliberately set out to create chaos for everyone. But in his fear of harm and his inability to accept himself where he was in his journey, he made a huge mess for himself and for everyone around him.

For those of us who once led fairly controlled lives, it is quite a shock to ourselves and others when everything flies out of our control and we can't rein it in, no matter how hard we try. This is the darkness before the dawn. And my mess was getting darker all the time.

I raged bitterly at people I loved and pumped myself full of enough anesthetics to make it through each day. I was terror-driven and made self-destructive decisions, but I stayed on the run so that no one could figure out my patterns, take me by surprise, and hurt me. My crazy thinking processes were de-

THE DUCKLING WAS AFRAID

signed to lead everyone off my track. In my journey I learned that I could use my messes to distract, manipulate, and deceive others. Not to hurt them, but to distract them just enough to keep some distance between them and me. This way people never knew me well enough and could never get close enough to hurt me.

It worked for a time. Of course, I made sure that the messes I showed to the world were socially acceptable ones. My excuses? "Single parenting is just too overwhelming. My kids are totally out of control." "I can't quit eating. I'm getting so fat." "I'm just not making enough money. We're getting deeper into debt all the time."

All the time, an internal mess was growing out of control, and the debris was becoming more visible as it spewed and overflowed into the external areas of my life.

I wish that, like Jesus, we could go to the cross, knowing somewhere deep within that what looks to everyone on the outside to be our ultimate destruction can actually turn out to be God's greatest victory. We never seem to make it to the place where, like the duckling, we give up and wait to die. This is the point we must come to in order to live. Jesus said, "unless a kernel of wheat falls to the ground and dies, it remains only a single seed. But if it dies, it produces many seeds" (John 12:24).

Jesus had to die in order to be resurrected. We, too, must die. But because we don't understand this part of the journey, and all we can see is the mess in front of us and darkness ahead, we live out our lives, simply adding to the mess as we go. We stay on the ground and don't let ourselves keep yearning after the swans. We don't try to spread our wings. We may not even know we *have* wings.

I have watched many ugly ducklings reach this point. They learn to manage their messes—they keep tidying them up, organizing them, and scrubbing them until they *look* spotless. They never break out, risk a flight, or move beyond lives of quiet desperation. But why?

The Shame

I woke up early that morning with a sick feeling in the pit of my stomach. I undressed and climbed into the shower. The sick feeling grew more intense. As I was ready to climb out a few minutes later, without warning, the sobs burst out from somewhere in my chest. I grabbed a towel and buried my face in it.

"No! No, no, no!" I had nothing else to say. "No, no! Oh God, no!"

I remembered the night before. I hadn't done anything wrong, but I had been tempted to. What was wrong with me? I had never before been tempted in the areas that were hitting me now. Why now? What was wrong with me? Something was horribly and terrifyingly wrong. Didn't the Bible say we are tempted by our own lusts (James 1:14 KJV)?

I had always considered myself a good person, a good Christian. During the thirteen years of my marriage, I couldn't remember even thinking a swear word. Now, not only was I thinking swear words, I was sometimes saying them out loud. And last night's temptation—well, what if the day came when it went further than thoughts? What if I gave in and acted on it?

Shame washed over me in waves as I stood in the bathroom that morning. I was ashamed of who I was and terrified of who I could become.

The sense of shame increased during the next few years as my life began to unravel. Threads trailed off in every direction faster than I could recover them and gather them together. Finally in touch with my pain, I lost control completely, flying into the milk pail, the butter bowl, and the flour barrel.

When I finally *"found a hiding place beneath some bushes,"* I knew I needed help. But I couldn't ask for it. I was too ashamed, and I couldn't possibly tell anyone about my mess, especially another Christian. The Christian women that I knew would never understand me. Everyone would just echo what I already believed about myself—I *was* rebellious.

Oh, I received unconditional acceptance from many of the

people around me. But they didn't really *know* me. And they never would. I would make sure of that.

Shame often causes us to hide, isolating ourselves to keep plenty of distance between us and others. The fear of being discovered drives us, and the only way we can break the cycle of shame is to begin to talk — to confess and release the pain to someone who cares and will listen without judgment.

Finding this person or group of persons is another matter. What made it especially difficult for me was that I could never admit that I needed anyone — for any reason. And the depth of my shame kept me on a surface level in most of my relation-ships.

But Barbara would not leave me alone. Actually, I can be quite charming when I need to be. She and I became friends during my charming moments. When my shadow side emerged, maybe she was in too deep. I'm not sure. All I know is that it was because I finally accepted this relationship that I knew I could probably tell her just about anything. I began to test her love.

I was too afraid to talk specifically about my mess. I began to drop hints, hoping she would pick up on them. She did. And even though things got worse before they got better, I know now that it was at that first moment of confession that my recovery began. This ugly duckling was about to catch a glimpse of her reflection.

I'm not talking about opening up to any old person. You can get into real trouble that way, like the ugly duckling did. Learn to recognize the swans, the ones who accept you where you are without value judgments, yet continually challenge you to plunge ahead. They won't impose their personal agen-das; they are interested in playing their God-given roles in your journey and in your ongoing growth and wholeness.

I want to be the person (swan, if you will) to whom others can come and release their shame. Because of my own wounds and my desperate need for acceptance in the midst of it all, I can hardly imagine anything that anyone could tell me that would make me turn away from them. Ugly ducklings (those who can acknowledge the depth of their ugliness) understand each other. We know there is no longer anything to hide. We are all in the same process of struggling to find our way, of discovering who we are and stumbling upon our reflections, even though we don't even know that's what we are seeking.

When our sense of shame penetrates deeply enough, the next step is to repent. By experiencing deep sorrow over our destructive and unloving actions, we will reach the kind of sorrow that eventually can change us.

The Depths of Repentance

Repentance is a word we hear so often in Christendom that I wonder if it has lost its meaning. Maybe the majority of Christians never understood it in the first place. I know I didn't. I imagine God's ideal to be that in the light of his holiness we could fully see our sinful selves. From a place deep within ourselves, we could truly experience the sorrow of falling so short of the mark.

But it doesn't usually work out that way. It was only through his horribly negative experiences that the ugly duckling could see the reality of his ugliness and how others viewed him. We must remember that we are all human and are all in the exact same boat. It seems that those of us whose ugliness becomes visible pay the highest price. We may be catalysts for those who, unaware of their own ugliness, are shocked when they see it surface in others and take it out on us.

We may also be catalysts for those who are aware of their own ugliness, but don't care. They take it out on us in order to keep the focus off of themselves. Either way, we seem to lose.

I am learning to live with that reality. In fact, I am now at the place where I even see this as a calling. If I cause other people's ugliness to surface by exposing my own, I can help them move closer to catching their own reflections.

This hasn't always been a conscious effort on my part. But I began to notice that when others saw my mess, they would wonder about their own. They could either choose to judge me for making a mess (and keep the attention off of themselves), or they could look at their own messes and begin to move through them. I discovered that most people were more interested in fixing *my* mess than in looking at their own.

As I began to understand repentance, it scared me almost as much as the danger of being harmed by others. To repent seriously meant I would have to take responsibility for the damage I had caused to others and to myself. It meant I would have to change. But how could I? I had never been able to change before.

What may look to us like an unrepentant person, bent on evil or self-destruction, may just be someone who has given up in despair. If you refuse to give up and if you have the determination to hang on, you may be the swan that glides by, saving an ugly duckling from death.

The Depths of Forgiveness

The act of repentance without receiving forgiveness leads to feelings of condemnation. Repentance alone isn't enough.

I did plenty of repenting as I flailed around in the debris scattered across my life. But I did it in private because I was so desperately trying to hide a mess that only seemed to grow in magnitude every time I turned around. The one friend who knew about my mess seemed to think I wasn't sorry enough. It bothered her that I was going about my life as if there wasn't a mess.

"Well, what do you want me to do?" I cried. "Go around in sackcloth and ashes?"

"You just don't seem sobered by any of this," she said.

I knew what she meant. Once again, I was overdoing it in the joke arena in order to cope. It looked like I wasn't taking my mess seriously. But she didn't see me as I writhed on my bed every night, crying out to God to forgive me and change me. Not a day passed when I wasn't deeply sorry for my sinfulness and how it affected others. But maybe she was right. I had to be sorrier. I had to repent more—experience more regret.

So I began to dig a hole for myself that went straight down to a pit of condemnation and false guilt. Look at how I had mismanaged my life. Look at how out of control it all was. I deserved to go to hell if that was what God decided.

This went on for a good two weeks before I realized what was happening. This wasn't *repentance*—an honest look at my sin and a deep sorrow that led to accepting God's forgiveness and deep, inner change. This was *condemnation*.

As children of God, we all claim to walk in the light of his forgiveness. However, in actuality, many lack understanding of what this means on a daily basis. When they sin or make mistakes that hurt God, others, or themselves, they don't repent. Instead, they:

- refuse to acknowledge it;
- try to cover it up;
- act like it is no big deal;
- justify it; or
- blame it on someone else,

when what they need to do is:

- repent;
- be sorry; and
- desire change.

I so admire and respect those who, when caught in a sin, are able to admit it and say to those involved: "I'm sorry. I was wrong. Please forgive me."

Receiving acceptance and receiving forgiveness go hand in hand. When we feel accepted by someone, we feel safe enough to ask for forgiveness when we blow it. Likewise, when we blow it in a relationship, experience forgiveness, and the other person doesn't leave us, we begin to feel safe and can receive acceptance.

The apostle Peter made many mistakes in his relationship with Jesus. He refused to let Jesus wash his feet (John 13:8). He rebuked the Lord for talking boldly about his death (Mark 8:31–32). He took matters into his own hands and cut off the High Priest's servant's ear (John 18:10). Three times he denied that he even knew Jesus (John 18:17, 25–27). And these are only a few cases—incidents we know about. Each time Jesus accepted Peter where he was, as a human being prone to weak moments and sin. Each time Jesus forgave Peter.

Without receiving acceptance and forgiveness, we lose our grip on relationships. If we can't receive, we have nothing to give, nothing to offer others in their journey to becoming swans. If we judge ourselves harshly, we also judge others. When we are unable to receive forgiveness because of the shame in admitting our sin, we immediately render ourselves ineffective in assisting other ugly ducklings in catching their reflections. Some people spin around in this cycle all their lives.

We must somehow break the cycle and let the truth of who we are penetrate.

Letting the Truth Penetrate

How could the ugly duckling possibly see anything true or good about himself when everywhere he turned, he was ridiculed and put down simply for being who he was?

Isn't this true for most of us? We can't see beyond the mess we have made of our lives, and, lest we forget, we have those who consider it their personal mission to remind us. Others always have opinions and ideas on what we can do to clean up our messes, the best way to go about it, and the amount of time it should take. And they are eager to share this information with us!

But there is only one truth that actually enlightens us in our journey toward becoming swans. That is the moment of revelation from God, the moment when we see our reflections, the real persons God created. When we see ourselves through God's eyes, we are magnificent swans indeed.

"But the duckling was afraid." Fear keeps us busy, keeps us distracted from the journey. It keeps us flailing around instead of calmly awaiting the moment when God is ready to unveil the truth.

What is the truth? The truth is that I am a swan. You are a swan. We are created in the image of God, but our ugly ducklings camouflage that swan much of our lives. God faithfully leads us to our reflections, but only *if* we stay on the journey.

Staying on the journey means to believe that, as the psalmist says, "I am fearfully and wonderfully made" (Ps. 139:14). It means that within the ugly duckling is a beautiful swan ready to emerge. I must believe this in order to stay motivated and keep moving. I need to learn to recognize God's hand in my life so that I can move in the direction he leads. I begin to stop blaming God for my pain and instead embrace it, realizing that the pain is necessary to move me forward in my journey.

To sum it all up, when I believe that God *is,* that he *accepts* me where I am, and that he *loves* me so passionately and madly that he will stop at nothing to prod me to that moment when I see the swan, then my beliefs will come full circle.

"It is I; don't be afraid," Jesus told his disciples (John 6:20).

I believe. I receive. It's that simple.

9

Spring Had Sprung

A Time to Hide and a Time to Appear

It would be too horrible to tell of all the hardship and suffering the duckling experienced that long winter. It is enough to know that he did survive. When again the sun shone warmly and the larks began to sing, the duckling was lying among the reeds in the swamp. Spring had come!

He spread out his wings to fly. How strong and powerful they were! Before he knew it, he was far from the swamp and flying above a beautiful garden. The apple trees were blooming and the lilac bushes stretched their flower-covered branches over the water of a winding canal. Everything was so beautiful: so fresh and green. Out of a forest of rushes came three swans. They ruffled their feathers and floated so lightly on the water. The ugly duckling recognized the birds and felt again that strange sadness come over him.

In the swan process, spring is the time when ugly ducklings recognize who they are and the power in their wings. It is also the time when those ugly ducklings who have been frozen on ponds begin to thaw out. But they may already have perished.

The key is to get to the ugly ducklings, frozen or almost so, before they die. I was one of those ugly ducklings who should have died. To this day, I'm not quite sure how or why I was able to navigate the waters of repentance and at last recognize my reflection. I looked dead. I acted dead. I was so numb, I could no longer feel the pain of being frozen.

But the swans came anyway. I think God sends them, whether or not we recognize them.

I was preoccupied when they first appeared. I was in the last stages of dying, and preoccupied with it. But preoccupation never stopped God before. It didn't this time, either.

I tried lifting my wings. I could fly—just a bit. It was a baby step, but a step just the same. The important thing was that God knew when to send the swans to me. And the swans knew when to appear.

The question, then, is whether we know when to appear for one another. "There is a time for everything" (Eccles. 3:1). There is a time to hide, and a time to appear. Part of the process of becoming a swan is knowing *when* to do *what* for the ugly ducklings in our lives. To hide when it is time to appear, or to appear when it is time to hide, may be to abort the swan process in another.

Romans 8:1 tells us, ". . . there is now no condemnation for those who are in Christ Jesus." Jesus is a Redeemer. He redeems our errors of bad timing. Still, playing the role of a swan who appears in someone's life is not something to be taken lightly.

Sometimes I get tripped up. Since discovering my reflection, I want to push everyone I know into this process. I fly above them in the sky, waving red flags so they're sure to see me. Too often I get angry if they choose to stay depressed, in denial or in fear of moving. But the truth is that, most often, I shouldn't even have appeared yet.

If we can ask God to give us a glimpse of his purpose for the ugly ducklings in our lives, we can ensure that our timing will be more in line with our Father's. The ducklings will then fly—not prematurely, to impress or please us—but because they are ready. It will be their time.

Why am I so eager to get everyone moving? What is it about us that pushes when we should be waiting for God's perfect time? Can we ever accept that, like it or not, life *is* the journey?

The Pain of Waiting

A crucial part of helping one another is to hear from God when and where we are to appear in the sky—or if we are ready to fly at all.

Waiting to appear is so hard for me. Too often, when it is time to appear, I forego the graceful flight above an ugly duckling in process and opt instead for a fast dive-bombing run, flapping my wings wildly and squawking at the top of my lungs to make sure I'm heard. It's a terrible sight.

I'm learning that we have to take people where they are. And that always involves waiting. People change at their own pace—have you ever noticed?

"A time to search and a time to give up" (Eccles. 3:6). When I have completed my search, at least for the moment, I want everyone else to be done, too. Much to my chagrin, it hardly ever happens that way.

"You've got to get out of there," I warned my friend who was in a toxic and abusive situation.

"Maybe you're right. I don't know." My friend hesitated. "I've just always believed that God could change anyone, anything—"

"That's not the point," I argued. "You're the victim here. Your codependent issues are tying into—"

I was off on another psychological lecture, but my friend was no longer listening. I was dive-bombing. All she felt was pressure from me.

I need to quit dive-bombing. To wait and let her glimpse some things for herself. When I realized it was time for a quick retreat, I left her to eventually see it for herself.

Dive-bombing does get people's attention, so it's not all bad. But how much better to glide by and stimulate their longings for freedom!

Waiting can be painful. We may fear that if something doesn't happen immediately, it never will.

Perhaps we can't bear to watch a beloved ugly duckling hurt, or we believe it's our responsibility (now that we have our knowledge) to keep pushing.

Perhaps we have experienced a degree of swan awareness, and now we want that for everyone—immediately!

When I think of my own process, I realize that I left the henyard a mere nine years ago, and I've barely seen my reflection. *God, help me to offer compassion and grace to my fellow sojourners.*

We only increase our anxiety by thinking we know the most effective strategy for change in another's life. We can greatly reduce our anxiety by choosing to trust that God is the one who gives marching orders, and by listening to him moment by moment.

The truth is, we have learned some things in our own lives that we can share with others. But it's usually best to wait until we have noticed an ugly duckling's longing to be a swan. We gain the right to touch, speak, or give a nudge only when we have glided by a few times.

Believing When We're Not Seeing

As I moved through the ugliest of my ugliness, a friend would periodically verbalize her doubts about my swan process. At times I would watch her study me.

"You know, you seem sincere," she would say. "It's just that, well, the majority of the time you're venting and flailing, and it's hard to tell. But then suddenly your heart comes through and I see the real person."

The emerging swan. Most of the time she saw me running from the hunters, griping about all the cats and hens in the world, and flying into the milk pail. Still, she prayed for me and believed in me. Herself a swan in process, she found the courage and faith to hang on. Her reward? Every once in a while she would catch a little glimpse of the longing in my eyes, see the straining of my wings, and hear the yearning in my cries.

Jesus said, "Blessed are those who have not seen and yet have believed" (John 20:29). Once we hear from God that we are to be the cheerleader in another's life, the swan that glides by, it is probably a good idea to count the cost. Otherwise we may be tempted to bail out with the first big wave.

I have always felt that if every duckling had even one swan to touch his longing, he could valiantly face his painful swan process. It only takes one person to believe. Only one.

How do we keep believing in one another's processes when we see little movement, when the ugly duckling we have chosen to believe in seems not to care, or at times even acts abusively toward us?

We can ask God. He knows who is serious.

We can look for ongoing brokenness and repentance, even though they may seem sporadic.

We can watch for honesty—a willingness to take responsibility for one's own life, feelings, abusive behavior, craziness, and all.

We can study the heart. Is there a longing to touch the swan, to love and be loved?

We can listen to the cry. Do you hear a determination to move through the pain?

How do you know when it's time to back off, either temporarily or permanently?

- When you find yourself resentful at expending more time and energy than you want to give, or because of too many blocked goals for the other person.
- When you can no longer pray in faith, or are too tired to care anymore.
- When you know your heart is cold toward the other, or you reel restless and want to move on.

God gives us the choice—we can choose to glide by and periodically land on an ugly duckling's pond, or we can keep flying.

Loud Protest

The time to protest loudly may come less frequently than we think. There is definitely "a time to be silent and a time to speak" (Eccles. 3:7). But our speaking is often ineffective when it is only out of principle, not out of compassion. Hurting people usually already know the principles; these are often the source of their pain in the first place. When value systems clash with heart responses, we need to remember that these ducklings need compassion.

If we can't glide by without squawking at the top of our lungs, it might be time to reconsider gliding by.

So when is a loud protest in order? Is it ever?

It can be like the story of the boy who cried "Wolf!" If we go around constantly squawking and screaming at everyone for the way they are believing, feeling, and living their lives, they will learn to turn down the volume just as fast as we can quack. I have learned this the hard way. My squawking comes so naturally that when I feel strongly about something, I have to work hard at relating quietly and calmly. At times I have tried to excuse the damage my squawking does by saying, "That's just the way I am. I have to express myself. You wouldn't want me to psychologically injure myself by repressing it, would you?" That may work for a while, but eventually I have to take responsibility for the harm I may have caused others.

The easiest place to squawk seems to be with our kids. We may start squawking frantically when they ask a simple question about sex or drugs.

"Mom, I was just wondering—today in school we talked about sexually transmitted diseases—"

Squawk, squawk, squawk. And we're off. By the time we stop, the kid is long gone.

When someone is actually headed for the edge of a cliff, a loud flapping of our bill may be necessary. But what would warrant this kind of warning? I figure that I can legitimately protest when my loved one is:

- in a relationship where abuse is accelerating;
- being drawn into a doctrinal system that refuses to honor Christ's redemptive act on the cross; or
- indulging in self-destructive behavior.

Yet even when loud protests are necessary, they must be carefully timed.

I have a friend who is moving through a divorce. Yes, it's sad. A thirty-year marriage is ending. However, everyone's untimely squawking and flailing is intensifying her pain to the point where some days she can't even function. Her phone rings incessantly. Everyone thinks they know how she should live her life, and they want to be the first to tell her.

"Sarah, you've got to make them stop this," I said one day. "The time for protests was over a long time ago. Quit arguing with these people. Sit down and share your heart with them."

As soon as she did, the barrage of loud protests stopped. Most of their protesting was motivated by fear. When she defused their fears, they calmed down.

Quiet Tolerance

What a beautiful sound — the silent flapping of swan's wings, the ruffling of their feathers, the rippling splash as they float lightly on the water.

Jesus showed quiet tolerance to unbelieving Thomas when, after his death, he appeared to the disciples and said, "Put your finger here; see my hands. Reach out your hand and put it into my side. Stop doubting and believe" (John 20:27).

Jesus showed quiet tolerance to Martha when he appeared *after* her brother Lazarus had already died and said, "Take away the stone . . . .Did I not tell you that if you believed, you would see the glory of God?" (John 11:39, 40). Jesus received Martha where she was.

And Jesus showed quiet tolerance to Peter when, after the disciple's third denial, "The Lord turned and looked straight at" him without saying a word (Luke 22:61).

Jesus always takes us as we are. That doesn't mean he doesn't prod us on to greater things, but he does that only after he accepts us in our present state.

One thing we can be sure of: the ugly ducklings of the world will always be testing us, pushing for a reaction, and wanting to know how much of them is OK with us. How wonderful it is to be the one to assure them that *all* of them is OK!

Yes, God grieves as he watches the pain we suffer on our individual journeys. But because God knows we will discover our reflections at the end, he is able to share his joy as well as his grief with us. Quiet tolerance is part of God's joy.

One of the scariest times of my life was when I had to stop reading the Bible for a while. Whenever I opened it and read any verse, I felt condemned. I had only recently come out of my spiritually abusive marriage, and through my damaged filtering system, I could only hear the Scriptures screaming at me in rage.

In order to find healing, I had to walk away from God's precious love letters to me and come back later with a different perspective. No one I knew at the time would have understood this, and so it was a very lonely part of my journey. But just as the ugly duckling honestly admitted to the cat and hen that he liked to float on the water, put his head under, and duck down to the bottom, I would sometimes be halfway into a conversation before I would catch myself.

"I'm not reading the Bible right now," I would flatly state. "It condemns me."

I remember a friend's wonderfully tolerant answer. "Then don't," she told me. "You don't have to give God anything right now." I stared at her, aghast. Here was quiet tolerance from someone who understood. No explanations were necessary. No defense needed to be made. She got it. I tend to think that quiet tolerance is the order of the day unless God gives us specific instructions to protest loudly. If I'm going to err, I'd rather err on the side of grace and mercy than of judgment.

Time to Fly

"So if the Son sets you free, you will be free indeed" (John 8:36). Is there a time to float and a time to fly? Nothing is wrong with floating, as long as we know when it's time to fly.

When the longing persists, gently pressing against the walls of our hearts; when we gaze into the sky and feel akin to the magnificent birds gliding by; and when our wings flutter, restless to the point of aching, then we know that God is calling out the swan.

Often we do the most damage to each other at this point in the swan process. It's a precarious time, for we must believe in the power of our wings to lift us. At such a time we can also offer wonderful encouragement to others, as long as we're aware of where they are on their journeys.

Knowing when *we're* ready to fly is one thing. How do we know when another is about to be thrust into flight?

The ugly duckling may pull away from anything familiar or refuse all assistance, no matter how lovingly it is offered. The duckling may question all formerly held beliefs and values, perhaps smile a little crazily at times, or even have a gleam in the eye that you've never seen before.

If you're watching and listening, you'll know. Swans understand timing. They knew the exact time to move toward me. Not a moment too soon and not a moment too late, they were there. And another swan was about to be born.

10

He Was a Swan

Bonding with Your Reflection

And he lighted on the water and swam toward the magnificent swans. When they saw him they ruffled their feathers and started to swim in his direction. They were coming to meet him.

"Kill me," whispered the poor creature, and bent his head humbly while he waited for death. But what was that he saw in the water? It was his own reflection; and he was no longer an awkward, clumsy, gray bird, so ungainly and so ugly. He was a swan!

It does not matter that one has been born in the henyard as long as one has lain in a swan's egg.

"I don't need you!" I screamed at my best friend, the very best friend I had ever had. "I don't need anybody! You hear me? I've made it this far all by myself . . . ."

My friend stood on my front porch and stared at me with the saddest brown eyes I'd ever seen. But I didn't stop. "You don't care, anyway. No one has ever cared . . . ."

The sobs tore at my throat, but I choked them down. I wouldn't cry. No way.

"I'm sorry," she said quietly. "But you do need me."

"No." And I shut the door, leaving her on the porch.

This was becoming a regular occurrence. The gut-wrenching pain in my life was affecting everything and everyone, every day. And I was exhausted from trying to keep it under control in order to live my life, raise my kids, and do my job.

Of course, I was sorry the minute I slammed the door. I mean, how much abuse can one person take? Would she stand there for a while and then ring the doorbell, or would she abandon me? I played games like this with people—daring them to abandon me. But this particular friend never did. No matter how many times I slammed the door, she always came back—knocking, waiting, loving. I guess that's what it takes—one person who truly understands God's unconditional love and can pass it on to hurting ugly ducklings like me.

Team Effort

It's hard work helping to bring out the swan in one another. We take lots of blows, bump up against many walls, and trip over countless obstacles—all so that one little ugly duckling on the planet can find his reflection.

Everything builds up to that one moment when we know that God loves us, and that because of God's love, we have inestimable worth. Knowing this gives us a very real and significant role in one another's lives.

The recovery movement has helped untold thousands of people find healing. But what concerns me is that, if we're not careful, it can distance us from one another even more. We are taught about boundaries, caretaking, people pleasing, victimization, and taking care of ourselves—to the point where I see myself as "the good guy" and everyone else as the enemy that is trying to get control of me in some way.

We do need to take care of ourselves, and we need to go through our personal recovery processes. But when we see taking care of ourselves as the entire goal, we miss the point.

The most important goal is to love. We learn to take care of ourselves only so we can love better.

When Jesus said, "Love each other as I have loved you. Greater love has no one than this, that one lay down his life for his friends" (John 15:12-13), he probably wasn't thinking about our little care-taking, people-pleasing, non-boundary-setting selves. The message of Jesus Christ has always been a simple one: to love, that our joy "may be complete" (v. 11) and that we might bear "fruit that will last" (v. 16).

To lead others to their reflections brings the greatest joy, and without a doubt brings forth fruit that lasts. For once we glimpse our true reflections, we are never quite the same.

The Clear Stream

To me, a clear stream symbolizes an open channel to God. How can we see our reflections when the water is murky and muddy? How can we clear the stream so that our reflections come through in sparkling, vibrant color?

Since this process takes place deep within our souls, where only God can reach us, ugly ducklings usually have to move away from the mob to discover their swans.

I see three key ingredients as being necessary for us to break through to that moment of touching our reflections—stillness, solitude, and serenity. The ugly duckling had to quit flailing and quacking, get off by himself, and come to a place of peaceful surrender to whatever fate awaited him.

1. Stillness. I have never been more aware of how much noise is filtered through our ears on a daily basis. Even as I write this, a train is rumbling and crashing along its tracks in front of me, while speeding cars whiz by behind me. And I'm at the beach, where I hoped I might find some quiet.

In church the other day, our speaker asked us to sit and meditate in total silence for two minutes. One hundred and twenty seconds. It felt like an eternity, and no one knew quite what to do with themselves. We discussed it afterward. Even though *externally* we stopped racing, we found it extremely difficult to still our thoughts. Left with nothing else, they shot off in every direction.

I'm working hard to cultivate silence in my life. With five kids, this is quite a challenge. But it was my frazzled existence that actually drove me to seek silence. And it wasn't until I found out how necessary silence was that I glimpsed my reflection.

2. Solitude. We're afraid to be alone. Does being alone suggest that no one loves us? That we're not worth spending time with? That we're easily discarded? Those are the reasons for *my* fear of solitude. We can handle solitude better when it's our own choice. Lately, I've tried to *choose* being alone. No one forces it on me by leaving me — I force it on myself, because I know it's essential for my ongoing emotional, psychological, and spiritual growth.

I don't know about you, but I'm finely tuned to my external environment — how it smells, feels, and appears. Whenever I'm in a crowd, I'm aware of how it's affecting me and I'm affecting it. I find it difficult to practice solitude in a crowd, although I want to learn how to do that. I don't want to always have to *leave* people in order to leave people, if you know what I mean. They're too precious. And we need each other. So I'm learning to manage their influence on me.

3. Serenity. After all his troubles, the duckling came to a place of peaceful surrender. He acknowledged his ugliness, and in so doing, he gave himself up to what he thought would eventually be his fate. He made the only choice he knew how to make.

We humans like to have peace before we make a decision. It makes the decision, whatever it is, feel more "right." However, I find that peace often comes *as* we make a decision. The act of making the decision is often what brings the peace. Whichever comes first, we won't be able to catch our reflections in waters that are troubled. When we accept our ugliness and let go of the duckling, the water will become crystal clear.

Letting Go of the Duckling

God can do little that is new in our lives unless we're willing to let go of the old. But how do we let go of the ugly duckling when that is who we *are*? My suggestion is not that we let go of the duckling, but that we let go of our *perception* of the ugly duckling.

In order to fully catch my reflection, to really grasp the fact that Christ's redemptive power is what makes me a swan, I had to first acknowledge and accept my ugliness and utter sinfulness. That familiar scripture, Romans 3:12, became a reality for me: " . . . there is no one who does good, not even one."

It is impossible for us to let go of our perception of the ugly duckling if we refuse to acknowledge just how ugly he is. He isn't ugly because of *who* he is—the reason that the henyard crew, the cat, and the hen rejected him. But he is ugly in how he presents himself to the world—in his fierce need to protect. For in that all-consuming intent to protect himself, he has no energy left over to love his world. We can't reach out to others when we're in our self-preservation or survival mode.

My main concern in my own survival mode was the daily struggle of trying to feel well enough just so I could get out of bed each morning. An honest look at how self-centered we can become in that mode is partly what thrusts us out of it.

To let go of our perception of our ugly duckling selves, we need to practice three things: determination, courage, and anticipation.

Determination. First of all, we have to want to move forward in the journey. If we're content to wander around outside the henyard all our lives, dodging hunters' bullets and dogs' jowls, crashing into milk pails and butter bowls, and running from excited children, then God will let us do that. Satisfied with being the ugly duckling, we will never choose to see our reflections.

Only the ugly ducklings who are determined to attain the

abundant life that Jesus promised will ever stop long enough to gaze into the clear stream.

Courage. It takes courage to move out of the familiar arena, the one we have known all our lives, and fly with the swans. The ugly duckling revealed what he was made of at the first crack of the egg, but especially when he fled the henyard, along with everything and everyone he had ever known. By refusing to settle for an abusive and "toxic" situation, he was already on his way to seeing his true self.

Anticipation. It's too hard to let go of our perception of the duckling when we have nothing else to look forward to. It's not necessary that we know exactly what it is that we're looking forward to, only that there is something—a goal, a destination (specifically, becoming a swan)—even if we don't know quite how we're going to get there.

Can we do it? Is it possible? Can we just believe that if we let go of our pain, our ugliness, and our roles as victims, that the joy of the revealed swan really awaits us?

The moment when we see our reflections in the clear water really does await us. We have only to believe.

Moment of Reflection

Unlike the ugly duckling's experience, for most of us the "moment" of catching our reflection is not a moment at all, but something that happens over a period of time.

What exactly is it that we catch? What is involved in this experience? What happens in this miraculous, magical moment?

- We know the depth of God's love, and this knowledge awakens our deepest feelings.
- Life's meaning and our life's purpose explode into focus—we know who it is that God created inside our physical shells.
- We love others because we are loved.

All this and more happens when we decide that we have had

enough and are ready to move on to the swan. The ones who touch their swans are the ones who will pay any price, and give their very lives, if necessary, to gain the pearl of great price.

Of course, most of us don't even realize that there's a reflection to be found. And once we do, we still have to be willing to move through all the pain outside of the henyard. There can be plenty of it.

The recent film "Thelma and Louise" aroused strong reactions in audiences. Many of the people I talked to saw it only as a movie that started with murder and ended with suicide. But I saw more than that. I also saw two women who were coming to life. At one point, Louise told Thelma, "You get what you settle for."

Something in me wasn't willing to settle for a life of ugliness. There had to be more. So I pushed on, through the pain of living, the meaningless relationships, the process of discovering the one true God. I met more hunters, dogs, hens, and cats than I care to count. But then I caught a glimpse of a swan in the sky. Such longing I felt—it would overwhelm me at times. To fly like a swan—to *be* a swan!

I had friends:

- one who was writing a book on fear, and as research, parachuted out of a plane;
- another one who courageously faced a brain tumor and triumphed; and
- another who recognized childhood sexual abuse and confronted her father.

I read books:

- *The Cinderella Complex* by Collette Dowling
- *Inside Out* by Larry Crabb
- *Homecoming* by John Bradshaw

I listened to music:

- "Running the Race" by Dallas Holm
- "Wind Beneath My Wings" by Bette Midler
- "Can't Slow Down" by Lionel Richie

I went to movies:

- "Dead Poets Society"
- "Silkwood"
- "Hook"

One thing I love about God is that he uses whatever we give him. He communicates with me in a variety of ways, as long as I'm listening.

For me, the moment I caught my reflection actually took place over a period of a few years. But with God, a thousand years are like a day. I figure he's always right on time.

The Swan's Egg

At some point we must recognize that we began inside the egg of a swan. This may be the most crucial part of the process. For if we don't recognize or understand from whence we came, and see our potential from God's point of view, we will miss the moment of reflection. The opportunity will present itself, maybe even more than once, but will pass quietly by without us even noticing. How God must grieve when this happens. The world is a sinful place: a henyard. But as M. Scott Peck writes in *The Road Less Traveled,* after his opening statement that "Life is difficult,"

> *This is a great truth, one of the greatest truths. It is a great truth because once we truly see this truth, we transcend it. Once we truly know that life is difficult—once we truly understand and accept it—then life is no longer difficult. Because once it is accepted, the fact that life is difficult no longer matters.*[1]

To me, the swan's egg symbolizes the deep, inner knowledge that in spite of our ugliness, we are truly created in God's image, and destined to become swans.

I remember the night I first clearly saw my ugliness. I truly repented. Buckets of tears flowed. But I had already met the man I would soon marry, and he was already telling me: "Christians don't sin. We're 'new creatures' in Christ. Perfect." "We might be tempted, but we don't have to give in. The Bible says, 'Be ye therefore perfect as your Father in heaven is perfect.'" "Light can't fellowship with darkness; as Christians, there's no darkness in us. We're perfect." "Anyone born of God does not continue to sin—1 John 5:18. That's because we're perfect."

He really believed this. What a delusion! And I bought into it—all of it. My knowledge of my ugliness quickly vanished, and I proudly and arrogantly raised my head and didn't lower it again for years. I strutted around the henyard, pecking at ugly ducklings who couldn't get their acts together, never seeing that my own self-righteous act was taking me farther and farther from the swan God intended me to be.

Like Moses, I spent much time in the wilderness. And to finally come to terms with it, I had to retreat all the way back to the broken egg, to see from whence I came, to allow myself to be completely deprogrammed—to enter the kingdom of God as a child, a new duckling, once again. But this time I became aware of my God-directed destination—some day I would be a swan. Whenever it became too painful, that is what I held onto. I would lose sight of it sometimes, and I didn't always believe it, but having encountered the cracked eggshell once again, I couldn't deny my destiny, no matter who lied to me or how painful the process became.

So, as important as recognizing our reflection in the clear stream is, equally important is never to lose sight of what we left behind when we entered the henyard.

The cracked shell. Eventually it leads to our reflection.

11

The Most Beautiful Bird of All

Rediscovering the Secret Each Day

> *He felt so shy that he hid his head beneath his wing. He was too happy, but not proud, for a kind heart can never be proud. He thought of the time when he had been mocked and persecuted. And now everyone said that he was the most beautiful of the most beautiful birds. And the lilac bushes stretched their branches right down to the water for him. The sun shone so warm and brightly. He ruffled his feathers and raised his slender neck, while out of the joy in his heart, he thought, "Such happiness I did not dream of when I was the ugly duckling."*

One of the interesting things about life is that we are all on the journey but are at different stages. To claim that once we touch our reflections, we are lovely and have arrived, is to believe the ultimate lie and to move into an arrogance as dangerous as the one we lived in before.

On the other hand, to fully acknowledge our loveliness is to honor our journey and God's work inside us.

Since glimpsing my reflection, I find that I still trip over many stumbling blocks—in some ways more now than before. I find myself less tolerant of certain ugly ducklings. Shouldn't recognizing my reflection enable me to offer more grace? I carry a huge weight of responsibility to teach everyone every-thing I know about this stuff. I must continually give this back to God so that I don't try to become chief caretaker of the world. I now love more, and therefore I grieve the world's sins that much more. I despise henyard abuse and find it difficult to love abusers. I find it difficult to own up to my compulsive sins because I feel I should know better than to have commit-ted them in the first place.

The more I know, the less I know—which brings frustra-tion.

The less I know, the more my questions increase—which causes insincerity.

And so it goes.

One thing that never changes is my absolute belief in God's love for me and the hope that he is the one in control of my journey. This is my safety and security.

Now that I can fly with the swans, I face the tendency to worry about being up too high, whether we're headed in the right direction, and what all of the animals in the henyard are thinking about us.

This journey hasn't come without its losses and pitfalls, that's for sure. I have lost a lot of friends. I have encountered much criticism. I have walked alone at times (and I *hate* feeling alone). I have jumped off emotional cliffs, not having the slightest idea if God would catch me. Like Paul,

> *I have been constantly on the move. I have been in danger from rivers, in danger from bandits, in danger from my own countrymen, in danger from Gentiles; in danger in the city, in danger in the country, in danger at sea; and in danger from false brothers. I have labored and toiled and have often gone without sleep; I have known hunger and thirst and have often gone without food; I have been cold and naked . . . . If I must boast, I will boast of the things that show my weakness (2 Cor. 11:26–27, 30).*

Paul was not after sympathy. He was boasting about his weaknesses, that he might show that God's power rested in him (2 Cor. 12:11). For the sake of Christ, he delighted "in weaknesses, in insults, in hardships, in persecutions, in difficulties" (2 Cor. 12:10). We all go through times of trial. The difference between ugly ducklings and swans is that swans understand the *purpose* of trials, and have stopped resisting so that they can more easily embrace the process.

Glad for the Hardships

Embracing the process means finally coming to terms with our henyard abuse, forgiving our abusers, and getting to the place where we actually feel grateful for having experienced *"so much want . . . so much suffering."* It really does mean that we can *"appreciate* [our] *present happiness and the loveliness of everything about* [us] *all the more."*

I remember how, one day a couple of weeks after separating from my husband, I was walking across a friend's kitchen, my arms filled with a stack of dishes to put away. My friend, who was headed across the kitchen in the opposite direction, threw open the cupboard door for me.

I stood motionless in the middle of the room while big teardrops formed in my eyes. She had been thinking of me. She wanted to make it easier for me. I couldn't believe it.

But it was such a small thing. Why had opening the cupboard door moved me to tears?

Nine years later it's still the same. Any kindness shown to me absolutely overwhelms me. I think those of us who have suffered abuse in the henyard or at the hands of hens and cats learn to expect more abuse. When someone treats us kindly, we are surprised and deeply moved.

I have often wondered if, after the abusive hardships are behind us, we would come to expect kindness again and repeat the cycle of disappointment and disillusionment.

It hasn't happened to me. The other day a guy let me in front of him in line at a gas station, and I resisted the spontaneous urge to reach out and hug him. His was a small gesture, but I could hardly hold back my expression of appreciation.

Jesus dealt with this issue when he graciously healed ten lepers and only one returned to thank him (Luke 17:11–19). It is true that too often we expect and demand that God do what we ask and give us what we need. I'm sure that the other lepers, aware of Jesus' power to heal, simply expected the Master to "do his duty." When, out of his abundant mercy and love, Jesus did so, they went merrily on their way, externally cleansed—but still demanding and self-centered. Internally they were unchanged. The thankful leper was one who had met Jesus internally as well as receiving external healing.

The fact that Jesus made an issue out of this incident means something. In his humanity, Jesus must have felt hurt when only one out of ten returned to thank him. My guess is that this leper had endured and accepted his present state, not like a martyr or victim, but bravely, not letting it embitter him. Having no expectations, his healing came as quite a surprise, and his gratitude overflowed.

The ugly duckling who refuses bitterness and comes to accept and embrace his journey is taken completely by surprise when he looks down to see his reflection. All ducklings have reflections—but few leave the henyard to seek them diligently.

Catching your own reflection is such an awesome moment that all of our past abuse is put into perspective and we are filled with undeniable gratitude and praise. We really can't help it, for we know that without the abuse, we wouldn't have started searching, and we certainly wouldn't have left the henyard and found our reflections.

This moment brings unbelievable happiness, but not pride, because *"a kind heart can never be proud."*

Never Proud

To me, a kind heart is simply a heart that, having acknowledged its ugliness, is now living in the light of its reflection.

True kindness only comes through constantly trusting Jesus, resisting the desire for self-protection, and choosing to reach out and love the world.

Pride becomes less of a problem *after* the moment of reflection than it was before. The reason for this is that swans know they have nothing to be proud of. The ugly duckling inside the swan is an ever-present reminder. Swans can only be proud of the process *God* has taken them through, the beauty *God* has created in them, and the wings *God* has given them.

As a new Christian, I thought I was hot stuff. I had obediently responded to the Holy Spirit. Didn't this place me a step above all the sinners who were still in the dark, unaware of their spiritual process? I boldly proclaimed John 3:18 to my mother, letting her know she was definitely one of the "condemned" and I wasn't.

At my ten-year high school reunion I announced to anyone who would listen that I was "saved," and I asked what important thing *they* were doing with their lives.

I stood tall and thanked the Lord for choosing me out of all the other "robbers, evildoers, adulterers" (Luke 18:9–14).

I was definitely proud of my "perfection"—until my life began to unravel. And then there was nothing in myself to be proud of anymore.

When I say that pride becomes less of a problem for the ugly duckling who has encountered his reflection, I am assuming that this ugly duckling is living with a sense of reality about himself. The reason the Pharisees had such a pride problem was that they had not looked realistically at their own depravity. As long as the outside of the cup was clean, they could fool themselves about the inside.

"So, if you think you are standing firm, be careful that you don't fall!" (1 Cor. 10:12). I know that I can take a healthy kind of pride in the swan that God has created in me. I also know that the minute my chest feathers pop out, I'm done for. That would defeat the whole purpose—God's purpose—and I couldn't bear to do that. So the very minute I am tempted to stand too tall, fly too high, or smile too broadly, I remember the duckling—and my own ugliness. Then the temptation toward sinful pride is gone.

Other problems loom. One of the more serious is *doubt*.

When in Doubt

Doubt plagues me.

On my especially ugly and depraved days, I doubt my relationship with God.

On my confusing days, I doubt my ability to think clearly, sometimes even to the point of doubting my sanity.

On my insecure days, I doubt my lovableness.

Every once in a while, I have a worry-free day. Most days, though, I am filled with doubts of one kind or another.

To see one's reflection and begin to understand the essence of life as a swan is not to become Godlike—all-knowing. No, what the swan does is make us "real."

And doubts assail the one who is real.

"Maybe I just imagined my reflection—it was a cloudy day, after all."

Or, "Was that really my reflection? Maybe it was someone else's."

Or, "*Reflection?* What reflection? I feel like I'm back in the henyard."

Like poisoned darts, doubts sail toward us at unbelievable speed, especially right after we glimpse our reflections. This is when we are the most vulnerable, because we don't yet trust our ability to see clearly, and we don't trust our wings to carry us. Most tragically, we don't trust God to tell us the truth about who we are.

In and of themselves, doubts are not bad. It's where we let our doubts take us that gets us into trouble. Doubts, worked through, can strengthen our faith. What keeps us from working through them? Fear. The minute doubts surface, we deny their existence and run. But running is only a temporary escape. Running from the henyard didn't solve the ugly duckling's problems. They only escalated, until at last he encountered his reflection—the moment he was created for.

Our doubts will only escalate if we try to pretend they don't exist. No, the way to handle doubts is to boldly confront them, wrestle them to the ground, and put a stake down before we take one step away.

We don't have to panic because we experience a doubt from time to time. The first step of the confrontation is really quite simple: "The only reason I can boldly confront my doubts is because God said I was a swan. So there." Once we really know and believe what God says about us, it is just a matter of reminding ourselves of the truth from time to time.

And if the doubts don't leave, wrestle with them.

To wrestle with our doubts is to embrace them, to honor them, and to give them the recognition they deserve. For example, the thought, *I'm not really a swan. Who have I been kidding all this time?* often shoots through my mind. I remember a time when some kids threw an egg at my van. I slammed on my brakes, tore out of my van, chased them up to their house, banged on their door, and demanded that they come out and clean it up. Sheepishly, they did.

Now, I may have had a right to be mad, but really—was that gracious swan behavior? Do swans acts like that? You better believe that was a doubting day for me!

So I ask myself questions like these:

- Does getting mad mean I didn't really see my reflection after all?
- I'm still a sinner. Does this mean that God has reduced my rank from swan to worm?
- I'm a nothing. Don't swans act like *something?*

The truth is that God's feelings about me and responses to me don't change just because there are times when I act like an idiot. Am I ever glad that God is more predictable than I am!

God loves me—wherever I am, all the time, and in spite of whatever I do. My doubts will never change that.

Stroking the New One

The other swans recognized the new swan and stroked him with their beaks. New swans need lots of stroking; they're unsure of themselves, wondering what it is that has happened and how it will change their lives. They are so used to the pecking and the roughing up that they hardly know how to respond to stroking.

Stroking comes in many forms. Just the presence of another swan is sometimes enough for us to feel the effect of the stroking. Sometimes it is enough to know that another swan is out there somewhere.

One of the most wonderful strokings I received from another swan came shortly after I had glimpsed my reflection. She spoke these words to me: "Now remember—no matter what anyone says, your authority is the Word of God *inside of you.*" Inside of me? I gasped internally, if not outwardly. I had been programmed never to trust what I heard inside of me, that it was sinful, terrible, and rebellious. I started listening more closely to my inner voice—carefully at first, then eventually taking in whatever it wanted to say to me. I began to celebrate this inner part of me. Call it my intuition, my heart, discernment—whatever. I rejoiced because I knew that now I could trust it. Not before, but now. It is one of the benefits that comes with honoring your reflection.

One can't overestimate the importance of stroking others as they seek to discover their swans. Criticism zings in from all sides, because most people simply don't understand the journey. Many refuse even to believe there is such a thing. I have often thought that I was crazy, that I made all this up or something. My kids continually say to me: "What are you doing? None of my friends' moms are into loving, forgiving, growing, and all that stuff."

At times like that, what gives me courage is the knowledge that I'm not alone on this path, that others have seen their reflections, and known that life has purpose, meaning, and significance. Don't be afraid to stroke the swans you discover.

- Tell them they're OK.
- Walk with them for a while.
- Remind them not to give up when the obstacles are looming.
- Cheer them in their growing, pray for them when they're detouring.
- Trust God when their journeys look vastly different from your own.

The Ongoing Journey

A few years ago, no one could have told me that I would ever actually enjoy life again, that my pain would turn into productive growth, and that my life would connect with others' lives in a significant way. As I waited on the pond for the swans to kill me, like Job I cursed the day of my birth (Job 3:1). Catching a glimpse of my reflection and discovering what God had truly created in me came as a total surprise. For the first time in my life, I am living. Living in reality. Living productively. Living passionately the abundant life that Jesus promised.

None of us knows how long our journey will be, how long we have to figure it all out. We may waste years in the henyard before we realize that we can't grow there. We may spend way too much time running from hunters and vicious dogs, never understanding that there is something better if we would but stop and look at what God has created. We may stubbornly refuse to leave the old woman's house, determined to get the approval of the hen and the cat.

Our lives take many interesting twists and turns. The good news is that when we become aware of the journey of the swan, they at last take on meaning. It's all for a reason. And it is oh, so worth it.

In God's eyes, there is no one too ugly, no one too peculiar, no one too big. The ugly duckling said, *"Such happiness I did not dream of when I was the ugly duckling."* We can't forget the ugly duckling. We can never leave him behind. We must hang onto the memories, the images, and the feelings. Too many other ugly ducklings are still out there and need us to remember the desperation and despair. When they lose hope we can hope for them.

God has created each and every one of us for the moment of reflection—that moment when we breathe a huge sigh of relief and realize that life isn't over, after all. It has only just begun. *"He was a swan! It does not matter that one has been born in the henyard as long as one has lain in a swan's egg."*

I watched a mother emotionally abuse her teenage daughter the other day and thought, *Inside of that mother is the most beautiful of the most beautiful birds.* My own daughter did some weird and abusive things this week, but I have to remember that inside of her lives a swan. A swan lives inside of you. A swan lives inside of me. A swan.

My prayer for you is that you will never again look at a swan in exactly the same way, that every time you encounter one, you will remember what you were created to be, and that you will honor God's creation—the swan in you.

Epilogue

*T*he most beautiful of the most beautiful birds' final words in the story are, *"Such happiness I did not dream of when I was the ugly duckling."* As in all fairy tales, we can assume that our duckling friend "lived happily ever after."

I believe that fairy tales do come true.

Are you wondering what I'm talking about? Who lives happily ever after? Anyone you know?

I think God has placed a rhythmic kind of hope inside us that the storytellers of many different eras have grabbed hold of: we are born, we hope, our hopes die, and then we live out one of two endings to our fairy tale—either our hopes die a complete death, never to be resurrected, or they are rekindled and burn eternal. We live happily ever after.

The Christian's fairy tale (except that it's reality) starts out with, "In the beginning God . . . " (Gen. 1:1) and ends with, "The grace of the Lord Jesus be with God's people. Amen" (Rev. 22:21). It is only because of God's grace that our fairy tale can have a happy ending. Happiness (true joy) does not mean the absence of problems and conflicts. But God so graces us with his deep, abiding presence that we are able to live above—to transcend—the problems, and find real purpose and meaning in this process.

I will never forget the agony and sense of despair that was my life before I discovered the secret of the swan. I have now integrated the painful memories into my life experience, but

God's gift through me is never to forget them completely. For my memories are what motivate me to prod others to embark on the journey—a journey that leads to the deepest and most satisfying relationship with God and others.

The other night, as I was flying in a plane above the stately Rocky Mountains of Colorado, I asked myself three questions: Where do I want to live? What do I want to do? and, Who do I want to love? (A little reevaluation from time to time never hurts.)

By the time my plane was flying in the night sky over Seattle, I had also realized three things: I was living where I wanted to live, doing what I wanted to do, and loving those I wanted to love. I'm on the journey, and I can celebrate the process. That wild, uncontrolled restlessness is a thing of the past.

I will always live with a certain amount of restlessness and pain, because I am not yet at my eternal destination. And so adjustments in my life may be necessary from time to time. But I know that the destination is God, and what he has prepared for me there is so glorious that no amount of happiness here can touch it.

I will be forever thankful to the ugly duckling for helping to prepare me for that place, for helping me touch my longing for the Swan—for God, the only one who can truly satisfy the longing of my heart.

Such happiness is yet to come.

Notes

Chapter 1

1. Max Lucado, *No Wonder They Call Him the Savior* (Portland, Ore.: Multnomah, 1986), p. 156.

2. Charles R. Swindoll, *The Quest for Character* (Portland, Ore.: Multnomah, 1987), pp. 202, 203.

3. *The Seattle Times*, August 7, 1988.

4. Gary Inrig, *Quality Friendship* (Chicago: Moody, 1981), p. 175.

Chapter 2

1. William F. Arndt and F. Wilbur Gingrich, *A Greek-English Lexicon of the New Testament and Other Early Christian Literature* (Chicago: Univ. of Chicago, 1957), p. 724.

2. John Fischer, *Real Christians Don't Dance* (Minneapolis: Bethany, 1988), p. 124.

3. Walter Anderson, *The Greatest Risk of All* (Boston: Houghton Mifflin, 1988), p. 2.

4. John Fischer, *Real Christians Don't Dance*, p. 144.

Chapter 3

1. Larry Crabb, *Inside Out* (Colorado Springs: NavPress, 1988), pp. 116, 117.

2. J. Keith Miller, *Sin: Overcoming the Ultimate Deadly Addiction* (San Francisco: Harper & Row, 1987), pp. 25, 16.

3. Luci Swindoll, *Alchemy of the Heart* (Portland, Ore.: Multnomah, 1984), p. 165.

Chapter 4

1. M. Scott Peck, M.D., *The Road Less Traveled* (New York: Simon & Schuster, 1978), p. 15.

2. John Fischer, *Real Christians Don't Dance,* p. 119.

3. Max Lucado, *No Wonder They Call Him the Savior*, pp. 161-62.

4. William F. Arndt and F. Wilbur Gingrich, *A Greek-English Lexicon*, pp. 459-61.

5. Daniel Taylor, *The Myth of Certainty* (Waco: Word, 1986), pp. 123-24.

6. Larry Crabb, *Inside Out*, p. 81.

Chapter 5

1. Tim Hansel, *You Gotta Keep Dancin'* (Elgin, Ill.: D.C. Cook, 1985), pp. 131-32, 136-37. Used with permission from David C. Cook Publishing Company.

2. Clinton W. MeLemore, *Honest Christianity* (Philadelphia: Westminster, 1984), p. 12.

Chapter 10

1. M. Scott Peck, *The Road Less Traveled,* p. 15.